LORENA GARCIA'S NEW LATIN CLASSICS

Fresh Ideas for
Favorite Dishes

LORENA GARCIA'S NEW LATIN CLASSICS

Lorena Garcia

with Raquel Pelzel

BALLANTINE BOOKS | NEW YORK

Published in the United States by Ballantine Books,
an imprint of The Random House Publishing Group,
a division of Random House, Inc., New York.

BALLANTINE and colophon are registered
trademarks of Random House, Inc.

ISBN 978-0-345-52543-7
eBook ISBN 978-0-345-53018-9

Printed in China on acid-free paper

www.ballantinebooks.com

2 4 6 8 9 7 5 3 1

FIRST EDITION

Book Design by Barbara M. Bachman

I dedicate this book to my mother, who gave me the strength and vision to view life in the best possible way and who made who I am today possible, as well as to all of the Latin Americans who have come to this country, fallen in love, and are proud to be called Americans.

CONTENTS

INTRODUCTION

· · · · · · · · · · ·

Love happens in the kitchen. It's in the comforting chicken soup you make for a friend who is under the weather. It's in the outrageously creamy pasta alfredo you cook for a girlfriends' night in. It's in the fish tacos you grill for friends picnicking on the beach and in the birthday cake you make from scratch for a child.

For me, cooking is the ultimate expression of love. Through a simple yet flavorful dish, I connect to friends and family in a way that shows them how much I care. It's the gesture of cooking and giving my time to help nurture someone else that is so touching and personal. The food doesn't have to be expensive or fancy; there's a reason why homey recipes like meatballs, pasta, chicken and rice, and guacamole are go-to comfort foods. No matter what your heritage or where in the world you live, giving the gift of a home-cooked meal is always met with appreciation and gratitude.

When I want to share comfort food, however, I have my own take, and what makes my take on these traditional American comfort foods different is the Latin edge, the twist of big and fresh flavors that I give it. I grew up in Caracas, Venezuela, and learned early on that the soul of Latin food is flavor. It's the punch of cilantro, the brightness of acid from freshly squeezed citrus, and the hit of heat from a jalapeño.

The one hundred–plus recipes in this cookbook will elevate everyday go-to dishes to a whole new level of flavor, because with Latin cooking, it's all about building levels of flavor—the depth of an onion, carrot, and bell pepper sofrito; the richness of homemade chicken stock; the edge of queso fresco. The flavors unfold as you take each bite—fresh, bright, concentrated, bold. This dynamic is what makes Latin food so deliciously irresistible.

My approach to modern Latin cooking is all about bringing a variety of global influences to the foods we love. Latin food is arroz con pollo (our famous chicken and rice one-pot meal) *and* chicken piccata. Arepas, tortillas, empanadas, ceviche, and tacos (of course!), but also soba noodles with ginger and soy, and pork loin stuffed with apples and walnuts with a vanilla mango sauce. Just as American food is more than burgers and apple pie, modern Latin food is more than tacos and guacamole.

Latin cuisine is a melting pot of cultures, and our face is one of many nations and lands. Our food expresses these beautiful influences—from China and Japan to Italy, Germany, and Africa, as well as the indigenous cuisine that goes back to the Aztec and Incan empires—but always with that unmistakable Latin influence. So if you're expecting just tacos and empanadas in this cookbook, you're in for a tasty surprise.

When I was growing up, I was lucky enough to get the best of both worlds—traditional Latin cooking and a taste for international cuisines. My mom worked full-time, and while she loved (loved!) to eat, she didn't have much time to cook. So I ate the food that my nanny, Leo, cooked. She made all of the comforting Latin standards—roast chicken, soups and stews, fresh corn arepas, and fideos, an angel hair–like pasta common throughout Latin America.

Mom had a job that required lots of international travel, and she often brought me along. By the time I was a teenager, I had had the unique opportunity to visit the countries from which many of South America's immigrants came, including Italy, Germany, and Japan, and to taste the food that people from those countries brought to Venezuela. I embraced the exotic tastes, and when I returned home, I would invite all of my friends over and cook them meals based on the many different flavors I had encountered: perhaps ravioli with four cheeses and a cream sauce, or maybe a stir-fry with marinated beef and loads of vegetables. Even before I knew I was all about food, I was all about food!

Though I always loved entertaining my friends and family by feeding them, the thought of being a professional chef never even crossed my mind; there weren't even any culinary schools in Venezuela. So I followed in my family's footsteps and went to law school, all the while hosting dinners and parties at my home. I continued to cook, travel, experiment, and be inspired. It wasn't long before I had successfully combined my two worlds, applying the basics of good Latin cooking—for example, punching up the flavor of a dish with a salsa—to recipes that came from around the world.

Shortly after I graduated from law school in 2000, my family and I moved to Miami. I continued to cook and entertain constantly, always keeping food simple and tasty, and letting the ingredients speak for themselves. Soon it was obvious that I was way more passionate about food than I was about law, and it wasn't long before an old family friend suggested I go to culinary school. Fast forward to one year later, and there I was, about to graduate from Johnson & Wales University—all I had left was to complete my internship.

During my last month on the job, I was frying a fish and the oil splashed up onto my face, scalding my skin so severely that I remained in the hospital for weeks recovering from the burns. Though I was emotionally and physically traumatized, I realized that I couldn't let my injury keep me from becoming a chef; I accepted my accident as a part of my educational journey. After being discharged, I hit the road, taking myself on a multicontinent tour of the best kitchens and cooking alongside some of the finest chefs in Europe and Asia. Through that experience, I defined my cooking style—modern Latin with a global twist—and soon started thinking about opening my own restaurant. After doing a lot of soul-searching, I returned to the States and made my dreams of being a chef in my own kitchen a reality.

By 2004, I had opened two successful restaurants in Miami, Food Café and Elements; hosted a TV show on Telemundo and on Univision's *Despierta América;* opened Lorena Garcia Cocina, my airport restaurant; and launched Big Chef, Little Chef, an initiative that educates families about eating healthfully in an effort to reduce childhood obesity. I also participated in CNN's acclaimed *Latino in America* series, which exposed me to an even-wider American audience. All of this led to an exciting NBC television show, *America's Next Great Restaurant,* and my first cookbook, a long-awaited and much-thought-about project that I am so proud of!

Through my experiences as a chef, my travels, and my encounters with home cooks facing everyday, real-life challenges, I have learned much. I turned to these experiences when I was writing this cookbook. For example, as you page through the recipes in this book, you'll notice a number of recurring items listed throughout the recipe ingredient lists. One major goal of mine was to not give people a huge grocery list and a pantry full of ingredients that wouldn't be used again. Being smart and economical, I decided to go for a common denominator of ingredients that would allow cooks to attempt just about any recipe in the book (most of the ingredients, by the way, are widely available in your local grocery store; see pages xiii–xix for these pantry items). By cooking your way through the basics of sofritos, stocks, and salsitas (to name a few), you can add an instant Latin vibe to just about any dish, from meat loaf to marinara sauce.

Like my cooking, the organization of the cookbook is untraditional. Instead of being divided into categories such as soups and side dishes, the organization is based on how I decide what to cook for a meal. I rarely sit at home and say to myself, "I need to make a chicken dish." No, instead I think, "My nephews are coming over tonight for dinner. They have huge appetites and will no doubt bring a group of friends. What will they want to eat?" For inspiration I would turn to the recipes in "*Cocina Casera*: Homestyle Favorites." Or, "I'm starving! I need to make something delicious, fast!" So I turn to "30 *Minutos*: Delicious Food on the Fly." or "It's so hot out I can't bear to turn the oven on. What can I make that doesn't require much preparation?" You'll find it in "*Afuera!* Move Your Kitchen Table Outside"—an entire chapter dedicated to dishes that require little effort and no stove-top or oven cooking. Cooking by occasion and circumstance is a great way to open yourself up to new ideas, and I think you'll find yourself trying out new dishes because they suit the cause. Additionally, each chapter includes starters, followed by entrées and sides, for ease of use. Dessert has a chapter devoted unto itself. Just in case you need it, you'll also find a recipe index in the back of the book that lists each recipe by its traditional category. Finally, *New Latin Classics* offers tips on stocking a *despensa,* or pantry, and basic recipes that the dishes in this book use as a flavor foundation.

Bringing Latin influences to the food you already know and love is going to offer a whole new world of possibilities for your cooking. From classic Latin dishes that get a modern update to homey American favorites presented with a Latin twist, I hope you will enjoy cooking from this global culinary journey as much as I did creating it.

Lorena Garcia

DESPENSA

What follows is a breakdown of select ingredients, most of which can be found in your local supermarket, that you should try to have on-hand in your *despensa* (pantry) to cook the recipes in this book. I didn't include every-day items like cinnamon, balsamic vinegar, salt, eggs, and butter (I consider the refrigerator and freezer to be as much of a pantry as the cupboards). What I did include are ingredients you might not have, like agave syrup and queso fresco, along with descriptions of what they are. And don't worry about buy-ing a whole bottle of hoisin and using it in only one recipe in the book. All of these ingredients are utilized in many of the recipes in this collection—a good Latina cook never lets anything go to waste!

DRY *DESPENSA*

AGAVE SYRUP: This neutral-flavored liquid sweetener is extracted from the spiky leaves of the agave plant (when agave is fermented, you get tequila). It is 40 percent sweeter than sugar, so you can use less of it in recipes that call for sugar; it is also completely vegan with a low glycemic index (good for those watching their carbohydrate intake, including diabet-ics), and a very neutral flavor. I like using agave syrup in sweet-savory sauces for meat, like in the Vanilla Mango Sauce for the Caramelized Apple and Walnut–Stuffed Pork Loin (page 83) and in vinaigrettes (see pages 74–75).

ARROWROOT: The fine white powder of a tuber, arrowroot thickens at lower temperatures than cornstarch and also isn't adversely affected by acid, meaning sauces, and especially citrus sauces, retain their bright, fresh flavor. It's great for adjusting the thickness of a hot or cold sauce. Just dissolve a little in cold water and add it in—it thickens immediately once you add it, so you know right away if you need more. I use it in the Chicken Albondigas with Lemon Piccata Sauce (page 151).

ASIAN CHILI SAUCE: I like adding semithick Asian-style hot sauce (like Sriracha Thai chili sauce) to my mango barbecue sauce for Mango BBQ Baby Back Ribs (page 119) and to Stir-fried Pork with Eggplant Picante (page 21). Made with spicy dried chiles and garlic, it's thicker and has a rounder flavor when compared to vinegary Latin- and Caribbean-style hot sauces and isn't overwhelmingly spicy.

BALSAMIC GLAZE: I save myself the step of having to reduce balsamic vinegar and instead buy balsamic glaze (*crema de balsamico*) in the supermarket. It is thicker and has a more caramel-y, subtle flavor than balsamic vinegar. Try pouring it into a squeeze bottle and using it to decorate a dish before serving the Sesame-Balsamic Sashimi Tuna with Wasabi Mayo and Baby Greens (page 69).

BEANS: Black beans are an absolute staple in the Latin pantry. You can find them in a range of recipes in this book, including Black Bean Soup with Bacon Sofrito (page 42), Black Bean and Jalapeño Hummus with Fresh Herb Drizzle (page 6), and Best Black Beans (page 205). I like to start with dried black beans, but you can substitute canned black beans if you're in a time crunch. One cup of dried beans yields about 2$\frac{1}{2}$ cups of cooked, canned beans (remember to rinse the canned beans under cold water before using).

CAPERS: The flower buds of a Mediterranean shrub, capers are briny and tangy. They're used a lot in South American cooking and come packed in either liquid or salt. Always rinse them under cold water before using. Great in the semisweet chimichurri sauce (see page 123) and they add that pivotal flavor to piccata sauce (see page 151).

CARIBBEAN JERK SEASONING: This is one of my favorite preblended seasonings. It works beautifully with grilled chicken (see page 113) and barbecued ribs (see page 119).

CHAMPAGNE VINEGAR: This high vinegar is made from the same grapes used to make champagne—pinot noir and chardonnay varietals. The fermented vinegar has a soft, vanilla-like flavor that I love in Tropical Passion Fruit Vinaigrette (page 75) and in Pollo con Passion (page 158).

COCONUT MILK: Coconut milk in a Latin cookbook? In South America, there is a huge Caribbean and Asian immigrant population, so yes, I cook a lot with coconut milk. I like how it adds body and a hint of sweetness to soups and broths, like the Butternut Squash, Coconut, and Lemongrass Soup (page 67) and the Clams and Mussels in Lemongrass Broth (page 9). Use light coconut milk if it's available—it adds the same flavor with less fat (a little goes a long way, too!).

DRIED FRUIT: Cranberries, raisins, currants, and other dried fruits add a nice sweetness; try adding them to braised meats or to add texture to a salad like the Quinoa, Sweet Peppers, and Fig Salad (page 144). Along with a healthy pinch of chopped fresh herbs, dried fruit breathes instant life into a bowl of Basic White Rice (page 204).

DULCE DE LECHE: When milk and sugar simmer for a long time in a saucepan, this magical sauce is the result. Thick and delicious, somewhere between caramel and butterscotch, dulce de leche is delicious on its own, poured over ice cream, or used to make Sticky Arroz con Dulce de Leche (page 182) or Mango Quatro Leches (page 189).

FISH SAUCE: Used throughout Asia in sauces, stir-fries, and as a dipping sauce, fish sauce adds a sweet-salty umami quality to food, similar to miso or soy sauce. It is made from fermented fish and/or shellfish, water, and salt and sometimes herbs and spices, too. It's great in the Stir-fried Pork with Eggplant Picante (page 21) and in the Sesame Soba Salad with Crunchy Vegetables and Herbs (page 13).

GRAINS: Rice is served in so many ways in South American cooking—with fried eggs, on the side with soup, as a salad, or refried. Of all grains, jasmine rice is my absolute favorite for simple steamed rice, but I keep a variety of different types in my *despensa,* including Arborio for risotto, brown rice, and long-grain white rice.

HEARTS OF PALM: Fresh is preferred, but canned works in a pinch. With a texture and taste similar to marinated artichoke hearts, canned hearts of palm are the actual soft-centered core of a palm tree, and make an exotic addition to salads and chilled dishes with tropical ingredients, like Tropical Sesame Shrimp Martinis (page 107).

HOISIN SAUCE: Sweet, sour, salty, and semithick and pasty, Chinese hoisin sauce is added to marinades (like the one for the Spicy Ginger and Orange–Glazed Chicken Wings on page 135) to give them an extra layer of fermented soy-plummy-garlic flavor.

MASAREPA CORN FLOUR: This flour is a must for homemade arepas. Since masarepa isn't treated with lime (nixtamal), it has a more subtle flavor than the masa used to make tortillas. Harina P.A.N., Areparina, and Doña Arepa are all good brands. The masa used to make tortillas, masa harina and Maseca, can also be used, but it won't yield a traditional arepa.

NUTS: Almonds, pistachios, and walnuts add texture, flavor, and protein to salads, rice dishes, and nut butters. If you buy them in bulk, store them in the freezer to keep them extra fresh for up to six months.

PANKO BREAD CRUMBS: These textured bread crumbs fry up with a light, crisp consistency (think tempura). I call for them in Grilled Sea Bass with Pistachio Crust and Tropical Passion Fruit Vinaigrette (page 81) and Tropical Crab Cakes (page 61).

PASTA AND NOODLES: Keep a bunch of different pasta shapes on hand (ditali, farafalle, linguine, orecchiette, rigatoni), as well as different pasta varieties, like noodles made from soba (buckwheat flour) and whole wheat pasta.

PINK PEPPERCORNS: These small peppercorns aren't really peppercorns, but rather the dried berries of the Baies rose plant that is native to South America. They are fruity and slightly peppery and are fantastic with sweet meats, like pork, or in the vinaigrette for the Cucumber Carpaccio (page 110).

PLANTAINS: These look like very large green bananas when underripe and very large black bananas when ripe. Green plantains are often sliced and fried, roasted, or mashed, and have a starchy texture and taste like a cross between an unsweetened banana and a potato. Ripe, black plantains are sticky-sweet and delicious fried and served with *nata* (sour cream). Perfect for baking (see page 206) or turning into a soup (see page 63).

RICE VINEGAR: A subtle, semisweet, and mild-tasting vinegar made from rice and used in Asian cooking. You'll find it in the wasabi mayonnaise for the Sesame-Balsamic Sashimi Tuna (page 69) and in the Lomo Saltado with Grilled Papayas (page 25).

RICE WINE (MIRIN): Made from fermented rice, rice wine adds a soft, sherry-like flavor to sauces and vinaigrettes like the one for the soba noodle salad (see page 13).

SESAME OIL: There are two varieties of sesame oil, light and dark (sometimes called toasted). Light sesame oil is mild, and dark sesame oil is stronger tasting and is best used as a finishing oil.

SOY SAUCE: This is a must in Latin American kitchens! Soy sauce brings an underlying savory quality to marinades and sauces like the glaze for the Pollo con Passion (page 158) and Lomo Saltado with Grilled Papayas (page 25).

SWEETENED CONDENSED MILK: Condensed milk gives a sweetness and consistency to desserts that is uniquely Latin and quite delicious. This canned and preblended combination of cooked milk with sugar gives great body and a light caramel flavor to Maruja's Flan (page 184), Fresh Berries and Golden Chocolate Sauce (see page 176), and Cappuccino and Biscotti Cups (page 174).

TRUFFLE OIL: A few drops instantly add sophistication to a pasta dish, compound butter, or risotto. Use it in Mango, Snapper, and Truffle Creviche (page 39), Truffled Salmon over Roasted Plantains (page 77), and Make-Ahead Wild Mushroom and Steak Risotto (page 89).

VANILLA BEANS: The seed pods of an orchid, vanilla beans contribute a floral quality to desserts and tropical sauces. They are sold whole as a pod, usually in a glass vial to keep the pod moist so you can slice it open and scrape out the seeds. In addition to using them in the Caramelized Vanilla Figs with Goat Cheese and Grilled Papayas (page 173), Creamy Peach Cups with Brûléed Peaches (page 179), and Vanilla Mashed Potatoes (page 87), I like to keep one in my sugar jar to infuse my sugar with a beautiful vanilla essence.

WINE: Like Chicken Stock (page 211) or Basic Sofrito (page 202), wine builds flavor fast. For cooking, I usually choose dry and citrusy-tasting pinot grigio or robust, fruity merlot or soft cabernet sauvignon when I need a red. Remember that you should cook only with a wine that's good enough to drink.

WORCESTERSHIRE SAUCE: We call this *salsa Inglesa,* or English sauce. It's very widely used in Latin America because it gives such great depth to sauces and marinades like the one for Short Ribs with Bay-Currant Sauce (see page 85). Made from a crazy combination of garlic, soy sauce, anchovies, tamarind, lime, and lots of other additions, it is a must-have.

YUCCA: Latins use yucca like Americans use potatoes. We fry it, steam it, mash it, everything! While fresh is best, if, in the frozen food aisle of the supermarket, you see yucca already peeled and par-cooked, go for it; it's a time-saver. This root vegetable, which also goes by the names cassava and manioc, has a brown, barklike, tough skin that must be peeled before you fry or boil it (see page 53). It has a mild, nutty flavor and a starchy texture similar to a baked russet potato.

COLD DESPENSA

AJÍ DULCE: Sweet and mildly spicy, this chile is about the size of a habanero and is often yellow-orange or red in color (a fresh pimiento) and is an important component of a balanced Basic Sofrito (page 202). If you can't find it, use a seeded, deveined jalapeño instead.

CILANTRO: This bright herb has a strong, clean taste. If you have an aversion to it, you can use parsley instead for a milder flavor.

CITRUS: Lemons, limes, oranges, blood oranges. Always keep a few of each on hand in the refrigerator for vinaigrettes, sauces, and salsitas.

FRESH GINGER: This root adds a bold kick to Asian-inspired sauces, salads, and broths and also to desserts. It has a knobby appearance and is covered with a paper-thin skin that must be peeled before grating or chopping. You can also peel ginger and freeze it to use later. It's a key ingredient in the Spicy Ginger and Orange–Glazed Chicken Wings (page 135) and Carrot and Ginger Soup (page 8).

GOAT CHEESE: Keep a little of this pungent cheese on hand for making salads like Spinach and Goat Cheese Empanaditas (page 33), or even to give a salty balance to desserts like the Caramelized Vanilla Figs with Goat Cheese and Grilled Papayas (page 173).

JALAPEÑOS: The workhorse chile of the Latin kitchen, a jalapeño can be mild, a little spicy, or very hot! To curb its fiery finish, split it lengthwise and scrape away the seeds and veins inside the chile before chopping. For a nice, smoky flavor, roast jalapeños in a 375°F oven for 30 minutes. Once they turn black, remove them from the oven, let them cool, and then slip off their papery skins. Place them in a shallow bowl, cover them with olive oil, and use within four days (use the amazing roasted jalapeño oil instead of olive oil whenever you want to punch up a vinaigrette for a salad or for drizzling over beans and grilled or sautéed vegetables.).

JICAMA: With the crunch of a crisp apple and a taste between an apple, pear, and red potato, jicama is a versatile root vegetable that I love adding to salads and salsitas (see page 195). It doesn't brown after cutting, making it a make-ahead-friendly addition for salads like the Chilled Shrimp and Peruvian Corn Salad (page 70) instead of apples.

MASCARPONE CHEESE: Creamy and decadent, mascarpone is an Italian cheese that is packed in small tubs. It is thick, similar to clotted cream, with a buttery silkiness and a sweet, creamy flavor. I love it on top of telitas (see page 131), used mixed in with or instead of ricotta in Prosciutto and Cilantro-Ricotta Spread (page 133), and in the Cappuccino and Biscotti Cups (page 174).

OLIVES: Black and green olives are a staple of the South American kitchen and should be in your fridge for salads, picadillo, or snacking. Green castelvetrano olives from Sicily and mild Gaeta olives are two favorites.

PAPAYA: Native to the Americas, this sweet-sour tropical fruit has a honeyed muskmelon taste and an incredible orange-pink color. Look for papayas that yield to slight pressure, or, if they are hard, let them sit out at room temperature for a few days to ripen. Split them lengthwise and scoop out the black seeds and discard before slicing and eating.

PARMIGIANO-REGGIANO CHEESE: The king of Italian cheeses, this cheese is made throughout the fertile Po Valley of Emilia-Romagna in Italy. It has a hard, granular texture with a deep, toasty, butterscotch flavor. Purchase it already grated, or buy it as a chunk and grate it fresh over pasta, risotto, salads, and grilled or steamed vegetables.

QUESO BLANCO: A firm white cheese that is good for grating over black beans or tacos. In many parts of South America, queso blanco and queso fresco (see below) are used interchangeably, but in Venezuela, queso blanco has a crumbly texture and flavor similar to a very mild feta or ricotta salata while queso fresco is more mozzarella-like in texture and flavor.

QUESO FRESCO: A medium-firm and sliceable fresh cheese with a tangy, slightly salty flavor and a mozzarellalike texture. While it softens when heated, it doesn't usually melt. It's excellent sliced and eaten with hot arepas.

TROPICAL FRUIT JUICES: Keep a container of mango, passion fruit, or papaya juice in the refrigerator. Perfect for a smoothie, vinaigrette, sauce, or dessert.

LORENA GARCIA'S NEW LATIN CLASSICS

30 *MINUTOS:* DELICIOUS FOOD ON THE FLY

In a perfect world, we'd all take our time in the kitchen cooking low and slow, letting sauces leisurely take on flavor on the stove top while a roast tenderizes for hours in the oven. However, my reality is probably a lot like yours, and I consider myself lucky to grab even thirty minutes in the kitchen to whip up a meal before collapsing on the sofa!

That's why I decided to devote an entire chapter to quick-cooking meals. The recipes in this chapter are the ones I created to work with my lifestyle and my tastes. They all offer wonderfully big, fresh flavors in a quick time frame: in under thirty minutes, to be exact.

Whether I'm at the end of a long day or hosting unexpected company, when it comes to food on the fly, usually I don't have much of a plan. I turn to salads, soups, quick seafood dishes, pasta, and stir-fries, using ingredients that happen to be in my fridge and *despensa* (see the pantry must-haves on pages xiii–xix). That's not to say that there aren't quick recipes in other chapters. These are different because they're my everyday favorites, the food I make when I need something comforting, satisfying, and fast.

TUNA TIRADITO *with* BLOOD ORANGE VINAIGRETTE

Serves 6

¼ cup Blood Orange Vinaigrette (page 75)

One 8-ounce sushi-grade tuna fillet, sliced crosswise into ⅛-inch-thick pieces

2 jalapeño peppers, halved, seeded, deveined, and thinly sliced

2 tablespoons finely chopped Candied Red Peppers (page 201)

1 teaspoon coarse sea salt

Tiradito is Peru's answer to sashimi and crudo. It's similar to ceviche except that the fish is sliced thinner and presented on a plate sprinkled with a vinaigrette-style sauce rather than a marinade. Typically there isn't any onion used in a tiradito (while onion is often in ceviche), but I like to add chopped shallots to the vinaigrette for sharpness. The garnet of the blood orange paired with the deep red of the tuna is absolutely beautiful.

Divide the vinaigrette among six plates. Lay a few pieces of tuna on each plate, shingling them one slightly on top of the other. Place a jalapeño strip on each tuna slice and follow it with a little of the candied peppers. Sprinkle each tuna slice with a little salt and serve immediately.

VARIATION: *Wild Salmon Tiradito*

Substitute fresh wild salmon for the tuna for a slight twist. If blood oranges are not available, try the tiradito with the Tangy Citrus Vinaigrette on page 74.

BLACK BEAN *and* JALAPEÑO HUMMUS *with* FRESH HERB DRIZZLE

Makes 1¹/₂ cups

1¹/₄ cups cooked black beans

2 tablespoons tahini sesame paste

1 jalapeño, halved, seeded, and finely chopped

¹/₂ small tomato, seeded and finely chopped

1 large garlic clove, halved

1¹/₂ tablespoons fresh lemon juice

1¹/₂ teaspoons sweet paprika

1¹/₂ teaspoons ground cumin

Pinch of kosher salt

¹/₃ cup extra-virgin olive oil

2 tablespoons Herb Drizzle (page 198)

Sliced Cheesy Telitas Flatbread (page 131), pita bread, or raw vegetables (such as carrot and cucumber sticks, cauliflower florets, and grape tomatoes) for serving

Black beans are one of the staple ingredients of South America because they are so very versatile, healthy, and affordable. In this recipe, the flavor of hummus is punched up with jalapeños, and traditional chickpeas are replaced with black beans. The hummus has a deep, rich color, wonderfully creamy texture, and a bright taste from all of the fresh herbs. Try it with tender telitas, on a sandwich instead of mayonnaise, or with raw vegetables. If you use canned beans instead of cooking your own (see page 205), be sure to rinse them under cold water first—it removes much of the sodium.

To make the hummus, place the black beans, tahini, jalapeño, tomato, garlic, lemon juice, paprika, cumin, and salt in the bowl of a food processor and pulse until well combined, using a rubber spatula to scrape down the sides of the bowl as necessary. With the machine running, drizzle in the olive oil, processing until the mixture is completely smooth and well combined. Scrape the hummus onto a medium plate and use the back of a spoon to smooth it out; make a small well in the center. Pour 1 tablespoon of the Herb Drizzle into the center of the hummus and drizzle the remaining 1 tablespoon over the top. Serve with telitas, pita bread, or raw vegetables.

CARROT *and* GINGER SOUP

Serves 4

12 cups Chicken Stock (page 211) or store-bought chicken broth

6 tablespoons unsalted butter

1 small yellow onion, roughly chopped

8 carrots, peeled and roughly chopped

One 1-inch piece fresh ginger, peeled and grated

1/3 cup all-purpose flour

1 1/3 cups cooked long-grain white rice (see note)

1 tablespoon kosher salt

1 1/2 teaspoons freshly ground black pepper

1/4 cup heavy cream

The secret to this totally elegant and creamy soup is to blend, blend, blend, which will result in a thick, voluminous, and silky soup.

1. Pour the broth into a large pot, bring it to a boil over high heat, and then reduce the heat to low.

2. Melt the butter in another large pot over medium heat. Add the onions and cook until they are soft and glossy, about 3 minutes. Stir in the carrots and ginger and cook, stirring often, until the carrots start to brown, about 5 minutes. Stir in the flour and cook, while stirring constantly (so the flour doesn't burn), for about 3 minutes. Pour in some of the hot broth a little at a time, stirring between each addition, until you have a loose, saucelike consistency, then add the rest of the broth and bring the soup to a boil.

3. Add the rice, salt, and pepper to the soup and cook until the rice is warmed through, 2 to 3 minutes. Turn off the heat and let the soup sit for 5 to 10 minutes, stirring occasionally to let some heat escape, before ladling one-third of it into a blender jar. Cover and pulse a few times to release the steam, and then puree the mixture until it's completely smooth. Pour the smooth soup through a fine-mesh sieve (or a cheesecloth-lined large-mesh sieve) into a clean large pot, using a rubber spatula to push it through. Repeat with the remaining soup.

4. Stir in the cream and cook for 2 minutes. Turn off the heat and serve.

NOTE: If you don't have leftover rice in the refrigerator, add 2/3 cup uncooked long-grain rice to the soup after adding the chicken stock and bringing it to a boil. Cook until it's completely tender (20 to 30 minutes) before cooling and blending.

CLAMS *and* MUSSELS
in LEMONGRASS BROTH

1 lemongrass stalk, trimmed

1 cup dry sake

1/2 cup light coconut milk

2 tablespoons bottled clam juice

2 carrots, roughly chopped

2 garlic cloves, roughly chopped

1 jalapeño pepper, halved, seeded, deveined, and roughly chopped

1 teaspoon kosher salt

2 dozen clams, scrubbed clean

2 dozen mussels, scrubbed clean

This dish is versatile and light, making it a great choice to start a meal. Clams and mussels are often some of the more affordable items in the seafood case, making this an economical dish, too. The sake, coconut milk, and lemongrass give the broth a very light, delicate, and distinctive flavor. For a more substantial meal, serve the broth with grilled, crusty bread.

1. Place the lemongrass on a cutting board and slice it in half crosswise, and then slice each half lengthwise. Turn the lemongrass quarters cut side down and use the back of a chef's knife to smash them in several places (this releases their lemony flavor). Set aside.

2. Place the sake, coconut milk, clam juice, carrots, garlic, jalapeño, and salt in a blender jar and puree until completely smooth. Pour the sauce into a large pot and add the lemongrass pieces, clams, and mussels. Cover the pot and place it over medium-high heat. Cook until the clams and mussels open, 6 to 7 minutes. Turn off the heat, uncover the pot, and discard the lemongrass pieces as well as any clams and mussels that didn't open. Divide the clams and mussels among four bowls, cover with lemongrass broth, and serve.

TOMATO BROTH *with* CLAMS *and* CRISP CALAMARI

Serves 4

5 tablespoons extra-virgin olive oil

2 whole dried red chiles

1 small yellow onion, finely chopped

½ small carrot, very finely chopped

½ small celery stalk, very finely chopped

3 garlic cloves, very finely minced

3 dozen small clams, scrubbed clean

½ cup dry white wine (such as pinot grigio)

One 8-ounce bottle clam juice

1 pound calamari, sliced into ⅛-inch-thick rings

2 cups Tomato Sauce (page 207) or store-bought tomato sauce

1 baguette, thinly sliced on a diagonal

Freshly ground black pepper

Fresh flat-leaf parsley sprigs for serving

While visiting my best friend from high school, who now lives in Capri, I tasted this incredible calamari dish: a thin yet intensely flavorful tomato broth served as the backdrop to flash-fried squid, crispy around the edges, inside tender and sweet. The chef threw thin rounds of fresh calamari into searing hot olive oil to scald the edges golden brown, and then he used the calamari instead of croutons to finish a bowl of tomato soup. This version is as comforting as the original, with a hint of spice from dried chiles and a deep tomato flavor thanks to the addition of homemade tomato sauce.

1. Heat 2 tablespoons of the olive oil in a large skillet over medium heat. Add the chiles and cook for 1 minute, then add the onions, carrots, celery, and garlic. Cook, stirring often, until the onions are soft, about 5 minutes. Add the clams and cook for 2 minutes, then pour in the wine and clam juice, cover, and simmer until the clams open, about 2 minutes. (Discard any clams that do not open.)

2. Use tongs to transfer the clams to a large bowl. Set a fine-mesh sieve over another bowl and strain the vegetables and sauce from the pan through the sieve. Discard the vegetables in the sieve and set the strained juices aside. Once the clams are cool enough to handle, remove the clams from the shells, discard the shells, and pour any accumulated juices into the bowl with the juices from the strained vegetables.

3. Heat 1 tablespoon of the olive oil in a large skillet over high heat. Add the calamari and the reserved clam liquid and cook the calamari until they turn crisp around the edges, about 2 minutes. Stir the cooked clams into the calamari and cook for

2 minutes. Pour in the tomato sauce, bring to a boil, and cook until the mixture reduces by half, about 10 minutes.

4. Brush both sides of the baguette slices with the remaining 2 tablespoons olive oil and sprinkle each with a little pepper. Preheat a grill pan over high heat or a broiler to high heat. Place the bread on the grill pan or on a rimmed baking sheet and under the broiler until browned, 30 seconds to 1 minute if pan grilling, 1 to 2 minutes if broiling (watch carefully as broiler intensities vary). Turn over the bread slice and repeat on the other side.

5. Divide the clams, calamari, and broth among bowls, finish with a parsley sprig, and serve with the toasted bread.

SOPA DE CHIPICHIPI

Serves 4

2 tablespoons extra-virgin olive oil

2 tablespoons unsalted butter

1 small yellow onion, finely chopped

1 large baking potato, peeled and cut into 1/4- to 1/2-inch cubes

2 carrots, finely chopped

2 celery stalks, finely chopped

6 garlic cloves, very finely minced

1 small shallot, very finely minced

One 1-inch piece fresh ginger, peeled and grated

1 cup dry white wine (such as pinot grigio)

3 cups bottled clam juice

2 dozen littleneck clams, scrubbed clean

1 dozen cherrystone clams, scrubbed clean

1/4 cup roughly chopped fresh cilantro

1 lemon, cut into 4 wedges

The flavor of this rich clam soup always reminds me of Sundays in Caracas, going to the beach and eating at a tiny corner restaurant where this dish was the specialty. In Venezuela, clams come in a huge variety of shapes and colors, making a bowl full of them steamed to tender perfection a truly beautiful thing. The clams cook in minutes—once they open, the soup is done. You can use any kind of clam—littleneck, cherrystones, or steamers, or even mussels if you prefer.

1. Heat the olive oil and butter in a large pot or Dutch oven over high heat. Add the onions and cook, stirring often, until they're translucent, 1 to 2 minutes. Stir in the potatoes and cook for 1 minute before stirring in the carrots, celery, garlic, and shallots. Cook until the shallots and onions are lightly browned, about 5 minutes. Add the ginger and cook, stirring constantly, until it's fragrant, about 1 minute.

2. Pour in the white wine and scrape up any browned bits from the bottom of the pot. Simmer for 1 minute and then pour in the clam juice and 1 cup of water. Bring to a boil, reduce the heat to medium, and simmer until the potatoes are tender, 6 to 7 minutes. Add the clams, cover the pot, and cook until the clams open, about 2 minutes. Turn off the heat, uncover the pot, and discard any clams that didn't open. Divide the clams and broth among four bowls. Sprinkle the cilantro on top and serve with a lemon wedge.

SESAME SOBA SALAD *with* CRUNCHY VEGETABLES *and* HERBS

Serves 4

1/4 cup soy sauce

2 tablespoons honey

1 tablespoon Asian chili sauce

1 tablespoon fish sauce

1 tablespoon fresh lemon juice

1 tablespoon mirin rice wine

1 tablespoon light sesame oil

FOR THE SALAD

One 8-ounce package soba noodles

2 tablespoons plus 1 teaspoon extra-virgin olive oil

1 yellow onion, halved and thinly sliced

6 garlic cloves, very finely minced

One 1-inch piece fresh ginger, peeled and grated

2 carrots, sliced lengthwise into thin strips

1 green bell pepper, halved, seeded, and thinly sliced

1 red bell pepper, halved, seeded, and thinly sliced

1 yellow bell pepper, halved, seeded, and thinly sliced

1/4 cup chopped fresh cilantro, plus 1 tablespoon for serving

1 tablespoon finely chopped fresh basil

1 tablespoon finely chopped fresh mint

2 tablespoons sesame seeds

If I need to feed people fast, the first place I go is the refrigerator to check out what I have on hand. If I have a nice selection of colorful fresh vegetables, then I make this soba salad. The key is to have all of your veggies and herbs ready to go before you start cooking—the dish moves along so quickly that you barely have time to stir between additions, let alone chop and slice. For an extra hit of protein, grill a chicken breast or some skirt steak, thinly slice it, and serve it on top of the salad. Substitute spaghettini if you don't have soba noodles. This salad is a great party item—divide it into mini Chinese take-out boxes and serve with chopsticks.

1. To make the sauce, whisk together the soy sauce, honey, chili sauce, fish sauce, lemon juice, mirin, and sesame oil in a medium bowl and set aside.

2. To make the salad, place a large bowl of ice water on the counter. Bring a large pot of water to a boil. Add the soba noodles and boil, following the package instructions, until the noodles are tender. Drain through a fine-mesh sieve and then plunge the sieve into the ice water to shock the noodles. Turn the noodles out into a medium bowl, drizzle with 1 teaspoon of the olive oil, and set aside.

3. Heat the remaining 2 tablespoons olive oil in a large wok or skillet over high heat. Add the onions and cook, stirring occasionally, until they're translucent, 1 to 2 minutes. Mix in the garlic and ginger and cook, stirring often, until fragrant, about 1 minute. Add the carrots and bell peppers and continue to cook until they're just starting to soften, about 3 minutes.

continued

Pour in $1/4$ cup of the honey sesame sauce and stir to combine.

4. Turn the soba noodles out into the pan and use tongs to toss them with the vegetables. Pour in the remaining honey sesame sauce. Turn off the heat and add the cilantro, basil, mint, and 1 tablespoon of the sesame seeds, using tongs to gently toss them with the noodles. Divide the noodles among four large plates, sprinkle with the remaining 1 tablespoon sesame seeds, and finish with some cilantro.

Sabes Qué?

Buckwheat soba noodles are a low-calorie and low-gluten alternative to pasta made from durum wheat. Some manufacturers make soba noodles with whole wheat durum flour so be sure to check the label if you're making the dish for someone with wheat sensitivities.

CHAR-GRILLED TUNA OVER PASTA
with CHERRY TOMATOES *and* OLIVES

2 cups small tube-shape pasta (such as ditali, pennette, or tubetti)

1 tablespoon plus 1 pinch kosher salt

1 tablespoon plus 2 teaspoons extra-virgin olive oil

1 tablespoon vegetable oil

One 14-ounce tuna steak

2 cups cherry tomatoes

1 large or 2 small garlic cloves, very finely minced

1/3 cup pitted picholine olives, roughly chopped

2 tablespoons brine-packed capers, rinsed

1 tablespoon finely chopped fresh ají dulce or jarred pickled cherry peppers

2 tablespoons Herb Drizzle (page 200)

4 scallions, white and light green parts only, thinly sliced

1/4 cup fresh basil leaves, stacked, tightly rolled, and sliced crosswise into thin strips

1/4 cup finely chopped fresh flat-leaf parsley

1 teaspoon freshly ground black pepper

Pasta salad is an excellent al fresco dish, great for picnics and beach trips. The trick is to load the pasta with big flavors so you get lots of complexity in each bite. Here the classic Italian dish pasta puttanesca has been transformed into pasta salad by quickly searing the tomatoes and fresh garlic in a pan, just enough to caramelize their sugars without losing the tomato's bright acidity and juiciness. Chunky bites of grilled tuna give this dish a smoky edge. Salty olives and capers, piquant chiles, and a bunch of fresh herbs send it over the top.

1. Bring a large pot of water to a boil. Add the pasta and 1 tablespoon of the salt and cook, following the package instructions, until the pasta is al dente. Place a large bowl of ice water on the counter. Pour the pasta into a fine-mesh sieve to drain and then submerge it in the ice water to shock it. Remove the pasta from the ice water, turn it out into a large bowl, drizzle with 2 teaspoons of the olive oil, toss to coat, and set aside.

2. Prepare a hot charcoal or gas grill.

3. Pour the vegetable oil into a small bowl and, using tongs, dip a folded paper towel (or a basting brush) into the vegetable oil and then rub the oil onto the grill rack. Place the tuna on the grill and cook until it is charred, about 1 minute. Use a spatula to carefully flip over the tuna steak and grill the other side until charred, about 1 minute longer. Carefully remove the fillet from the grill and set it on a cutting board and slice the tuna into 1-inch chunks. Set aside.

4. Heat 1 tablespoon of the olive oil in a large skillet over high heat. Add the cherry tomatoes and garlic and cook, stirring often, for 1 minute. Add the olives, capers, ají dulce, pasta, and

16 · LORENA GARCIA'S NEW LATIN CLASSICS

a pinch of salt and use tongs to toss to combine. Cook until the pasta is heated through, about 3 minutes. Add the tuna and herb drizzle and toss gently to combine so the tuna doesn't break up. Add the scallions, basil, parsley, and black pepper. Toss to mix, divide the pasta among six bowls, and serve.

GROUPER A LA PLANCHA *with*
SUN-DRIED TOMATOES *and* SPINACH

Serves 4

Four 6-ounce grouper fillets
1½ teaspoons kosher salt
1½ teaspoons freshly ground black pepper
1 tablespoon extra-virgin olive oil
4 garlic cloves, very finely minced
½ shallot, very finely chopped
⅓ cup dry-packed sun-dried tomatoes, thinly sliced
¼ cup dry white wine (such as pinot grigio)
2 cups spinach leaves
½ cup half-and-half
½ cup Chicken Stock (page 211) or store-bought chicken broth
1 tablespoon roughly chopped fresh flat-leaf parsley

Fish is one of my favorite fast foods. It's healthy and cooks quickly, plus its natural flavor allows it to pair with a range of different ingredients from mild to strong. Living in Miami, I'm lucky enough to have access to pristine, just-off-the-boat, locally caught fish, but if finding good-quality, firm, and fresh-smelling fish isn't a possibility in your area, buy frozen (flash frozen is best—it maintains the texture and flavor of the fish). If grouper is unavailable, switch it up with mahi mahi, snapper, or cod.

1. Season the grouper with 1 teaspoon of salt and 1 teaspoon of pepper and set it aside. Heat the olive oil in a large nonstick skillet over high heat. Place the grouper fillets in the pan and cook until browned, about 3 minutes (if you don't want the ends of the fish to curl, use a spatula to lightly press them down). Add the garlic and shallots and then carefully slide a spatula under the fish and flip it onto the other side.

2. Add the sun-dried tomatoes and white wine to the pan, gently adjusting the fish so some wine gets beneath it, and then add the spinach, half-and-half, and chicken stock. Bring the sauce to a simmer and once it begins to thicken, after about 5 minutes, stir in the remaining ½ teaspoon of salt and the remaining ½ teaspoon of pepper and turn off the heat. Divide the spinach mixture among four plates, top with the grouper, sprinkle with the parsley, and serve.

SHRIMP in ENCHILADO SAUCE

Serves 6

3 tablespoons extra-virgin olive oil

6 garlic cloves, very finely minced

1 large shallot, very finely minced

One 1-inch piece fresh ginger, peeled and grated

1 pound large shrimp (21 to 25 per pound), peeled and deveined

½ cup dry white wine (such as pinot grigio)

½ red bell pepper, finely chopped

¼ green bell pepper, finely chopped

One 14.5-ounce can diced tomatoes

½ cup canned tomato sauce (half of an 8-ounce can)

¼ cup Chicken Stock (page 211) or store-bought chicken broth

1 jalapeño pepper, halved, seeded, deveined, and finely chopped

1 cup bite-size broccoli florets

1 tablespoon finely chopped fresh basil

1 teaspoon kosher salt

1 teaspoon freshly ground black pepper

An enchilado sauce is typically made with lots of fresh and dried chiles and is quite spicy. This one is a balance of sweet heat due to the combination of mild-flavored red and green bell peppers for body, a little jalapeño pepper for heat, and the fresh taste of ginger (if you want it spicier, just add a pinch of crushed red pepper flakes). When it comes to cooking shrimp, take extra care with cooking time, as even an extra minute in the pan can turn sweet, succulent shrimp rubbery. This dish is delicious over mashed potatoes or Basic White Rice (pae 204).

1. Heat the olive oil in a large skillet over high heat. Add the garlic, shallots, and ginger and cook until fragrant, stirring often, for about 1 minute. Add the shrimp to the pan and cook until they just start to color, about 1 minute. Use tongs to turn the shrimp and cook the other side for 1 minute.

2. Pour in the white wine and cook for 1 minute. Stir in the bell peppers, tomatoes, tomato sauce, chicken stock, and jalapeño. Cook for 1 minute and then add the broccoli. Cover the skillet and cook until the broccoli turns bright green and is al dente, about 3 minutes. Stir in the basil, salt, and black pepper, cook for 1 minute longer, and serve.

STIR-FRIED PORK *with* EGGPLANT PICANTE

Serves 6

- 2 tablespoons vegetable oil
- 4 long, thin Asian or Italian eggplants, trimmed, halved lengthwise, and sliced into 1-inch-thick pieces
- 1 pound ground pork
- 1/4 cup rice wine
- 1/4 cup rice vinegar
- 1/4 cup soy sauce
- 3 tablespoons fish sauce
- 1 1/2 tablespoons Asian chili sauce
- 2 tablespoons sugar
- 1/4 cup finely chopped fresh cilantro
- 2 tablespoons sesame seeds
- 4 scallions, white and light green parts only, thinly sliced on the bias

Many years ago I visited Kyoto for several weeks, working in different kitchens to learn about Japanese flavors, foods, and cooking methods. While I didn't speak the language, I observed, watching how the chefs used ingredients and how they cooked. The effect on my cooking was powerful, and I developed a real love for stir-fries that feauture light, clean flavors prepared in simple, quick ways. This recipe reminds me of an Asian slant on picadillo (see headnote page 156), a classic Latin ground meat dish. This is perfect over Basic White Rice (page 204). Both fish sauce and Asian chili sauce can be purchased in Asian markets and are also commonly found in the ethnic aisle of large supermarkets.

1. Heat the oil in a large wok or skillet over high heat. Add the eggplants and cook until both sides are browned, about 10 minutes total. Make a well in the center of the eggplants (so the center of the pan is visible) and crumble the ground pork into the pan. Cook the pork, using a wooden spoon to break up any large pieces, until browned, about 10 minutes.

2. While the pork browns, whisk together the rice wine, rice vinegar, soy sauce, fish sauce, chili sauce, and sugar in a medium bowl. Pour the mixture over the eggplants and the pork, stirring to combine. Cook until the liquid is reduced by half, about 7 minutes.

3. Turn the stir-fry out onto a platter and finish with the cilantro, sesame seeds, and scallions.

SOUTH AMERICAN CHICKEN FRICASSEE

Serves 4

8 skinless, boneless chicken thighs

1 teaspoon kosher salt

1 teaspoon freshly ground black pepper

¼ cup extra-virgin olive oil

1 large white onion, finely chopped

3 garlic cloves, very finely minced

1 teaspoon tomato paste

¾ cup golden raisins

½ cup pitted green olives, thinly sliced

½ cup pitted black olives, thinly sliced

⅓ cup brine-packed capers, rinsed

Zest of 1 lemon

1½ teaspoons whole pink peppercorns (or less for a less pungent flavor)

1 green bell pepper, halved, seeded, and finely chopped

1 small tomato, cored and chopped

1 cup Chicken Stock (page 211) or store-bought chicken broth

One baguette, sliced, for serving

¼ cup heavy cream

Balsamic vinegar for serving

1½ tablespoons finely chopped fresh cilantro

For birthday parties and family gatherings, my nanny, Leo, always made this traditional saucy chicken fricassee. The flavor, with sweet raisins, salty olives, briny capers, tomatoes, and browned onions, is very Latin and gives the chicken a wonderfully complex taste, without much effort. I add a hint of lemon zest to brighten its finish, a drizzle of cream to make it extra rich, and a splash of balsamic vinegar to give it a touch of sweet-acid taste. Serve fricassee family style with mashed potatoes or white rice (see page 204) and fried plantains (see page 206), and, just as Leo did, expect to get requests for it for every family gathering.

1. Rinse the chicken under cold running water. Pat dry with paper towels, season with the salt and black pepper, and set aside.

2. Heat 2 tablespoons of the olive oil in a large saucepan over medium-high heat. Set the chicken in the pan and cook until both sides are golden brown, about 8 minutes total. Remove the chicken from the pan and place it on a large plate; set aside. Add the onions and garlic to the pan and cook until the onions are starting to brown, about 5 minutes.

3. Stir in the tomato paste and cook, stirring often, for 3 minutes before mixing in the raisins, green olives, black olives, capers, lemon zest, and pink peppercorns. Add the bell peppers and tomatoes, and then pour in the chicken stock. Return the chicken to the pan and bring the broth to a simmer. Cover the pan, reduce the heat to medium-low, and cook until the tomatoes break down, 5 to 8 minutes.

4. While the chicken is cooking, toast the baguette slices. Adjust an oven rack to the upper-middle position and heat the broiler to high. Brush both sides of the bread with the remaining 2 tablespoons olive oil. Place eight baguette slices on an aluminum foil–lined rimmed baking sheet and broil until browned, 1 to 2 minutes (keep an eye on the bread as broiler intensity can vary). Turn over the slices and toast the other side, 1 to 2 minutes longer. Remove the pan from the oven and set it aside.

5. Stir the heavy cream into the fricassee, cook for 1 minute to bring the flavors together, and turn off the heat. Place 2 slices of baguette on each of four plates. Top with 2 pieces of chicken and some sauce, drizzle with a little balsamic vinegar, sprinkle with cilantro, and serve.

LOMO SALTADO *with* GRILLED PAPAYAS

Serves 4

continued

FOR THE MARINADED BEEF

- 1 garlic clove
- 1/4 teaspoon kosher salt
- 2 tablespoons canola oil
- 4 teaspoons rice vinegar
- 4 teaspoons soy sauce
- 1 tablespoon oyster sauce
- 1 teaspoon ground cumin
- 3/4 teaspoon freshly ground black pepper
- 1/2 teaspoon sweet paprika
- 1 pound beef tenderloin, sliced crosswise into 1/4-inch-wide slices

FOR THE LOMO SALTADO

- 1 large papaya, halved and seeded
- 1 teaspoon vegetable oil
- 1 tablespoon extra-virgin olive oil
- 1 large red onion, halved and sliced 1/2 inch thick
- 1 cup halved cherry tomatoes
- 1/2 shallot, very finely chopped
- 3 garlic cloves, very finely minced
- 3/4 cup red wine (such as merlot)
- 2 tablespoons soy sauce
- 1 tablespoon honey
- 1/2 cup finely chopped fresh cilantro, plus a few sprigs for serving

Lomo saltado, sautéed tenderloin, is a classic Peruvian-style stir-fry of steak and onions (and sometimes bell peppers). We have a lot of Asian immigrants in South America, and this dish marinated in rice vinegar, soy sauce, and oyster sauce is a reflection of their profound influence on our culture. I serve it in a grilled papaya boat that adds a wonderfully tropical taste and stunning presentation. If you can plan ahead, take the time to marinate the beef overnight—the result is worth it.

1. To make the marinade, finely chop the garlic clove, sprinkle with the salt, and mash the mixture together with the flat side of a chef's knife. Continue to mash and chop until the mixture is a paste. Scrape the paste into a medium bowl and whisk in the canola oil, rice vinegar, soy sauce, oyster sauce, cumin, pepper, and paprika. Add the beef, turn to coat in the marinade, cover the bowl with plastic wrap, and set aside for at least 2 hours or overnight.

2. Prepare a hot charcoal or gas grill.

3. To make the lomo saltado, coat each papaya half with some vegetable oil and then place them cut side down on the grill, cooking the papaya until it has grill marks and is browned, 6 to 8 minutes. Use a spatula to transfer the papaya to a plate. Set aside to cool while you cook the steak. (Alternately, preheat the oven to 400°F. Place the oiled papaya halves in a grill pan cut side down and roast in the oven until the cut side is golden brown, 6 to 8 minutes.)

4. Heat the olive oil in a large wok or skillet over high heat. Once the oil starts to smoke, add the steak and onions and cook, stirring often, for 1 minute. Stir in the cherry tomatoes, shallots, and garlic and cook, stirring often, until the tomatoes start to collapse, about 4 minutes.

5. Pour in the red wine, soy sauce, and honey and cook until the sauce is slightly thick, about 4 minutes. Stir in the chopped cilantro. Cook for 2 minutes longer to bring the flavors together and then turn off the heat.

6. Place the papaya halves on a platter and divide the lomo saltado between the halves. Finish with the cilantro sprigs and slice lengthwise into wedges to serve.

VARIATION: *Lomo Saltado with Fries and Rice*

One of my favorite ways of eating leftover Lomo Saltado is tossed with French fries and over Basic White Rice (page 211)! It's a total carb-load but so delicious and satisfying—and actually quite traditional, too.

SPICY ORECCHIETTE VERDE

Serves 4

2½ teaspoons plus 1 tablespoon kosher salt

1½ pounds broccoli crowns, divided into small florets

1 pound orecchiette pasta

¼ cup plus 2 tablespoons extra-virgin olive oil, plus extra for serving

6 garlic cloves, very finely minced

2 large jalapeño peppers, very finely chopped (seeded and deveined for less heat)

1 shallot, very finely chopped

1 teaspoon minced fresh ají dulce or jarred pickled sweet cherry peppers

¾ teaspoon crushed red pepper flakes

1 cup grated Parmigiano-Reggiano cheese, plus extra for serving

3 large basil leaves, stacked, tightly rolled, and sliced crosswise into thin strips, plus 4 small sprigs for serving

1 tablespoon finely chopped fresh flat-leaf parsley, plus extra for serving

Pinch of freshly ground black pepper

Instead of using the typical basil for a pesto, I use tender, cooked broccoli florets to make this easy sauce. Nutty Parmigiano-Reggiano cheese gives it richness, and jalapeños and ají dulce chiles give it some bite!

1. Place a large bowl of ice water on the counter. Bring two large pots of water to a boil. Add 1½ teaspoons of the salt and the broccoli to one pot and cook until the broccoli is very soft, about 15 minutes, then drain it through a sieve and plunge the sieve into the ice water (this keeps the broccoli's color bright).

2. Meanwhile, add 1 tablespoon of the remaining salt to the other pot and then add the orecchiette. Cook, following the package instructions, until al dente. Drain the pasta (reserve ⅓ cup plus 2 tablespoons of the pasta water) and set aside.

3. Once the broccoli is completely cooled, remove it from the ice water and break it up into small bits. Set aside.

4. Pour ¼ cup of the olive oil into a large skillet and heat it over high heat. Add the garlic, jalapeños, shallots, broccoli bits, ají dulce, red pepper flakes, and 2 tablespoons of the pasta water. Stir until the mixture looks almost like pesto. Reduce the heat to medium-low and cook to warm the broccoli, about 1 minute.

5. Add the cooked orecchiette along with the remaining 2 tablespoons olive oil and the remaining ⅓ cup pasta water. Stir in the Parmigiano-Reggiano cheese, basil, parsley, the remaining 1 teaspoon salt, and the black pepper until the mixture is well combined. Divide the pasta among four bowls, sprinkle with additional cheese and some parsley, and finish with a sprig of basil and a drizzle of olive oil.

COCINA
CASERA:
HOMESTYLE
FAVORITES

In my eyes, what makes a dish a Latin classic is how it connects Latinos from different countries. Whether someone grew up in Venezuela or Argentina, Colombia or Peru, chances are pretty good that black bean or lentil soup or chicken and rice was often served at mealtime. Some recipes, like the corn cakes called *arepas*, can vary from country to country. In Mexico, corn cakes very similar to arepas are called *gorditas*, while in El Salvador, they are known as *pupusas*. Of course I fall back on the tender-cakey texture of the arepas I grew up eating in Venezuela. One of my favorite childhood memories is the sound of my mom slapping arepa dough into flat disks between her palms. Once I smelled the fresh-cooked sweet corn wafting out from the kitchen, I'd race there, ravenous and ready to eat more than my fair share.

While "Cremita di Apio" or "Reina Pepiada" may sound unfamiliar, once you look through their ingredient lists, you'll see that to make these traditional foods, you probably have all or most of the ingredients already stocked in your pantry (see pages xiii–xix for my must-have *despensa* list).

Of course I give the recipes my own twist, adding layers of flavor from smoky bacon, lots of fresh herbs, the punch of fresh citrus juice, and good olive oil. In this way I satisfy my expectations of bright and bold-tasting food simply prepared and create a modernized version of these very traditional dishes.

VENEZUELAN AREPAS

Makes 16 arepas

2 cups Doña Arepa, Harina P.A.N., or Areparina corn flour

1 tablespoon sugar

1 teaspoon kosher salt

4 tablespoons (1/2 stick) unsalted butter, melted

2 tablespoons vegetable oil

Unsalted butter, cream cheese, queso fresco, or mozzarella for serving

Light and golden corn flatbreads called *arepas* are an absolute staple at the Venezuelan table—they are to Venezuelans what baguettes are to the French. Morning, noon, and night, we eat them with everything from sweet butter to scrambled eggs and Carne Mechada (page 162). From the most humble kitchen table to the fanciest gourmet restaurant, when Venezuelans break bread it is fresh griddled and steamy arepas that they're ripping into.

These arepas don't veer far from tradition with one exception: In an effort to lighten up classic Latin cooking, I almost always bake my arepas instead of deep-frying them (I say "almost" because sometimes I fry smaller portions; see page 164). I brown the arepas on the griddle first to concentrate the flavors in the dough and get a great, crisp crust. Then they go into the oven, where they puff into tender corn cakes. Like biscuits, arepas are at their best fresh out of the oven, while they're still steamy and warm. Shaped and uncooked apreas can be wrapped tightly in plastic wrap and refrigerated for up to one day (the dough can also be refrigerated for up to one day; knead slightly to warm the dough before shaping).

1. Adjust your oven racks to the upper-middle and lower-middle positions and preheat the oven to 350°F.

2. Whisk together the corn flour, sugar, and salt in a large bowl. Set aside.

3. Whisk the butter into 2 1/2 cups of water, then add it to the flour mixture, stirring until well combined. The dough will start out loose but the flour quickly absorbs the liquid. Start to knead the dough in the bowl and once it becomes very soft and

doesn't stick to your hands, after about 8 minutes, the dough is ready to be shaped (if, while kneading, the dough seems too stiff and breaks apart, add a few tablespoons of hot water; if it is too sticky, add a little more corn flour).

4. Divide the dough into 16 equal balls and flatten each between your palms into a $3^1/_2$- to 4-inch patty that's about $1/_3$ inch thick (for a less rustic-looking arepa, press the arepa into a disk using a flat-bottomed plate; you can wet your hands with a little water if the dough is slightly sticky).

5. Heat 1 tablespoon of the vegetable oil in a large nonstick skillet over medium-low heat for 2 minutes. Add 3 or 4 arepas to the pan (depending on how big your pan is); the arepas should sizzle as they hit the skillet. Cook the arepas until they're golden and have a nice crust, 6 to 8 minutes. Flip them and brown the other side for an additional 6 to 8 minutes. Transfer the arepas to a rimmed baking sheet and set aside. Repeat with the remaining 1 tablespoon oil (if the pan is dry) and the remaining arepa dough disks (you'll probably need to use two baking sheets to bake the arepas).

6. Bake the arepas until they puff up, 20 to 30 minutes, switching the pans, so the top baking sheet is on the bottom and the bottom moves up to the top, midway through cooking. Remove from the oven and set aside for 5 minutes before serving with butter, cream cheese, queso fresco, or mozzarella.

continued

VARIATION: *Fried Arepitas with Nata*

Preheat the oven to 200°F. Divide the arepa dough into 36 balls and, using your palms or a plate (see page 30), shape the arepitas into 2-inch-wide and 1/3-inch-thick patties. Heat about 6 cups vegetable oil in a straight-sided, deep skillet (you should have 1/2 inch of oil in the pan). Fry the arepitas on each side until golden, 6 to 8 minutes per side. Transfer to a paper towel–lined plate and set aside for 5 minutes before serving with *nata* (sour cream) or queso fresco, mozzarella, or butter.

Sabes Qué?

The arepa dough can easily be made in a food processor. Just pulse the wet and dry ingredients together until they form a shaggy ball, then let the food processor run until the dough is semismooth. Turn the dough out onto your work surface and knead it by hand until it is malleable and doesn't stick to your hands, 2 to 3 minutes, then proceed as directed.

SPINACH *and* GOAT CHEESE EMPANADITAS

Makes 40 empanaditas

FOR THE SPINACH FILLING

- ¼ cup pine nuts
- 6 cups spinach leaves
- 8 ounces fresh goat cheese (about 1 cup)
- 1 tablespoon fresh lemon juice
- 1 tablespoon kosher salt
- 1½ teaspoons freshly ground black pepper

FOR THE EMPANADITA DOUGH

- 4½ cups all-purpose flour
- 1 tablespoon baking soda
- 1 teaspoon kosher salt
- 1 cup vegetable shortening
- 1 cup cold milk
- 2 large eggs
- 1 large egg yolk

Savory baked or fried turnovers can be found throughout the world—from Italy (calzone) to India (samosas) to the Caribbean (pastelitos). These crescent-shaped stuffed pastry dough pockets are a huge part of South American food traditions; we eat them any time of day, even for breakfast with a *cafecito* (little coffee). The variety of empanada fillings is really limited only by your imagination—if you have leftover roasted vegetables, meats, or even just ham and cheese in the refrigerator, you have the makings for a tasty empanada. This version, which is a modern interpretation, balances the toasty richness of pine nuts with sharp goat cheese and the brightness of fresh lemon juice with fresh spinach. I keep the empanadas small (empanaditas) and easy to eat for a predinner bite or afternoon snack.

1. To make the filling, toast the pine nuts in a small skillet over medium heat, shaking the skillet often, until they're golden brown, 3 to 5 minutes. Transfer to a small plate to cool.

2. Place a large bowl of ice water on the counter. Bring a medium pot of water to a boil over high heat. Submerge the spinach leaves in the boiling water and immediately remove them and place them in the ice water to stop the cooking. Remove the spinach leaves from the ice water and squeeze out as much water as you can. Place the blanched spinach in the bowl of a food processor and add the cooled pine nuts, the goat cheese, lemon juice, salt, and pepper and process until smooth, scraping down the bottom and sides of the bowl as needed. Set aside.

continued

3. To make the empanadita dough, whisk together the flour, baking soda, and salt in a large bowl. Add the shortening and, using a pastry blender or your hands, work it into the flour mixture until there are no pieces larger than a small pea. Whisk the milk with 1 of the eggs and the egg yolk and add it to the flour-shortening mixture, stirring with a wooden spoon until a dough ball forms. Cover the bowl with plastic wrap and refrigerate for 30 minutes.

4. Preheat the oven to 400°F.

5. Place a small bowl of water next to a lightly floured work surface. Whisk the remaining whole egg with 3 tablespoons of water to make an egg wash and set aside.

6. Divide the dough into 2 pieces and place 1 piece on the floured work surface. Roll it out into a $1/4$-inch-thick sheet. Use a 5-inch round cookie cutter to cut out as many dough circles as you can, keeping them close together to minimize the amount of dough scraps. Discard the scraps. Repeat with the remaining piece of dough. You should end up with about 40 dough circles.

7. Place 1 heaping tablespoon of the spinach filling in the center of each circle. Dip your finger or a pastry brush into the water and moisten the edge of the lower half of the circle. Fold the top half over the bottom half and press the edges together to seal. Crimp the edges using a fork and place the empanadita on a parchment paper–lined rimmed baking sheet. Repeat with the remaining dough circles and filling.

8. Brush the tops of the empanaditas with the egg wash and bake the empanaditas until golden brown, 12 to 15 minutes. Remove from the oven and serve warm or at room temperature.

BEEF, OLIVE, *and* RAISIN EMPANADITAS

Makes 20 empanaditas

4 large eggs

2 red potatoes, peeled

12 tablespoons (1½ sticks) unsalted butter

3 yellow onions, finely chopped

1 red bell pepper, halved, seeded, and cut into ½-inch pieces

1 pound beef sirloin, cut into ½-inch pieces

¼ cup golden raisins

2 bay leaves

1 tablespoon ground cumin

1 tablespoon sweet paprika

1 tablespoon crushed red pepper flakes

5 scallions, white and light green parts only, thinly sliced

1 teaspoon dried oregano

¼ cup finely chopped green olives

½ empanadita dough recipe (see page 33), rolled and cut into 20 circles

I'm always looking for an element of surprise when I bite into an empanada. I want to get a taste of every flavor and texture in each and every mouthful—from salty to tangy, sweet to bitter, creamy to flaky. This ground beef, olive, egg, and raisin filling combination is very traditional in South America. Depending on the region you're in, the filling can take on new players—in Medellín, Colombia, chorizo might be used instead of ground beef; in Bolivia, peas and carrots are often added; while in Chile, where meat is expensive, less beef and more onions are often mixed in. Feel free to adjust and experiment with the recipe as you like. It's hard to go wrong.

1. Place 3 of the eggs in a medium saucepan and cover with cold water. Bring the water to a simmer over medium-high heat and cook for 7 minutes. Transfer the eggs to a bowl of ice water, and once they are cool enough to handle, peel and slice them into small cubes.

2. Bring a medium pot of water to a boil. Add the potatoes and cook until a knife easily slips into their centers, 20 to 25 minutes. Drain the potatoes and set aside to cool. Once they are cool enough to handle, peel the potatoes and dice them into ¼-inch pieces.

3. Heat a large skillet over medium-high heat. Add 6 tablespoons of the butter, the onions, and bell peppers and cook, stirring often, until the onions are translucent and the peppers are tender, 5 to 7 minutes. Stir in the beef, raisins, bay leaves, cumin, paprika, and red pepper flakes. Add the remaining 6 tablespoons butter, cover the pan, reduce the heat

continued

to low, and cook until the beef is completely cooked through, 10 to 15 minutes.

4. Stir in the potatoes, scallions, and oregano and cook to allow the flavors to come together, about 2 minutes. Transfer the mixture to a large bowl and set aside to cool. Once the mixture is cool, discard the bay leaves and stir in the cubed eggs and olives. Cover the bowl with plastic wrap and refrigerate for at least 1 hour or overnight.

5. Preheat the oven to 400°F.

6. Place a small bowl of water next to a lightly floured work surface. Whisk the remaining 1 egg with 3 tablespoons of water to make an egg wash and set aside.

7. Place 1 heaping tablespoon of filling in the center of each dough circle. Dip your finger or a pastry brush into the water and moisten the edge of the lower half of the circle. Fold the top half over the bottom half and press the edges together to seal. Crimp the edges using a fork and place the empanadita on a parchment paper–lined rimmed baking sheet. Repeat with the remaining dough circles and filling.

8. Brush the tops of the empanaditas with the egg wash and bake the empanaditas until golden brown, 12 to 15 minutes. Remove from the oven and serve warm or at room temperature.

MANGO, SNAPPER, AND TRUFFLE CEVICHE

Serves 4

- 1 large sweet potato, peeled and sliced into 1/4-inch-thick rounds
- 3 1/2 tablespoons fresh lemon juice (from 1 large lemon)
- 3 1/2 tablespoons fresh lime juice (from 2 limes)
- 1 teaspoon truffle oil
- 1/2 teaspoon kosher salt
- 1/2 teaspoon freshly ground black pepper
- 1/4 cup fresh or frozen (thawed) mango chunks, chopped into small pieces
- 1 jalapeño pepper, stemmed and finely chopped (seeded and deveined for less heat)
- 10 ounces fresh red snapper fillet, skin removed, fish finely chopped into 1/4-inch pieces

At its most basic, ceviche is a classic Peruvian dish of raw fish that is marinated in lemon or lime juice (or both, as in this recipe) for as little as fifteen minutes or as long as several hours. The acid in the citrus juice changes the proteins in the fish—heat does the same thing to meat, which is why many people say that ceviche is "cooked," even though it never comes into contact with the heat of a grill or stove top. Ceviche is popular all over Central and South America and very simple to make. The most important ingredient is the fish, of course, so buy the freshest available. If red snapper isn't available (or doesn't look that great), you can use tuna, tilapia, shrimp, grouper, salmon, calamari, or even lobster instead. Remember: Fresh fish should smell sweet and feel firm to the touch. It should never be mushy or smell fishy. While it may seem unusual, sweet potato is actually a very traditional Peruvian accompaniment to ceviche. Here the sweet creaminess of the potato nicely counters the acidity of the sauce. (See photograph opposite.)

1. Place the sweet potato rounds in a microwave-safe steamer and steam in the microwave until tender, 8 to 10 minutes. (Or, bring 1 inch of water to a boil in a large pot. Place the sweet potato rounds in a steamer basket, cover the pot, and steam until tender, about 15 minutes.) Transfer the potato rounds to a plate and set aside to cool. Once they're at room temperature, cover the plate with plastic wrap and refrigerate until chilled, about 30 minutes.

2. Whisk together the lemon juice, lime juice, truffle oil, salt, and black pepper in a medium bowl. Stir in the mango chunks

continued

and jalapeño, then gently stir in the snapper. Cover the bowl with plastic wrap and refrigerate for 20 minutes.

3. To serve, place the sweet potato rounds in the bottoms of four bowls. Use a slotted spoon to divide the ceviche among the bowls and pour the remaining marinade over the tops.

Sabes Qué?

I find that the best way to ensure the fillets you're purchasing are fresh is to buy a whole fish and ask the fish-counter person to scale and fillet it for you. That way you can look at the eyes of the fish to make sure they're crystal clear and press the flesh of the fish to test its firmness (fresh fish should be tight and feel slightly firm to gentle pressure). Your fillets are guaranteed fresh.

TUNA CEVICHE *with* LECHE DE TIGRE

FOR THE LECHE DE TIGRE

- 1 carrot, roughly chopped
- 1 celery stalk, roughly chopped
- 1 small yellow onion, roughly chopped
- 1/2 cup fresh lemon juice (from about 3 lemons)
- 1/3 cup soy sauce
- 1 tablespoon coconut milk
- 1 teaspoon vegetable oil
- Pinch of kosher salt
- Pinch of freshly ground black pepper

- 10 ounces sushi-grade tuna, sliced on a mandoline or with a sharp knife crosswise into 1/8-inch-wide strips
- 1/2 small red onion, very finely chopped
- 1/4 small red bell pepper, very finely chopped
- 1/2 cup fresh cilantro leaves, chopped
- 4 endive leaves for serving (optional)
- Store-bought baked yucca chips or baked wonton chips, for serving (optional)

Leche de tigre is the name Peruvians give the marinade for ceviche because after sitting with the fish, the liquid turns a pearly, opalescent white reminiscent of milk (*leche*); the bite of the tiger (*tigre*) comes from the bold pop of acidic lemon or lime juice. The broth of a ceviche should be just as delicious as the fish in it. In this tuna ceviche, the juice gets an extra flavorful boost from coconut milk and soy sauce, giving it an Asian fusion taste. Endive spears are used here as edible spoons.

1. To make the leche de tigre, place the carrots, celery, onions, lemon juice, soy sauce, coconut milk, vegetable oil, salt, and black pepper in a blender and puree until completely smooth. Refrigerate for at least 20 minutes or up to 2 days.

2. To make the ceviche, gently toss the tuna with the onions and bell peppers in a medium bowl. Pour the chilled leche de tigre over the tuna mixture, add the cilantro, and stir gently to combine. Cover the bowl with plastic wrap and refrigerate for 10 minutes.

3. Use a slotted spoon to divide the ceviche among four martini glasses. Drizzle a little leche de tigre over each serving and finish with an endive leaf and some of the yucca chips, if using. Serve immediately.

COCINA CASERA: HOMESTYLE FAVORITES · 41

BLACK BEAN SOUP *with* BACON SOFRITO

Serves 6

2 cups dried black beans

6 cups Chicken Stock (page 211) or store-bought chicken broth

4 bacon slices, finely chopped

1 green bell pepper, halved, seeded, and finely chopped

1 cup Basic Sofrito (page 202)

10 garlic cloves, very finely minced

2 tablespoons ground cumin

2 bay leaves

Using home-cooked beans rather than canned makes all the difference with this simple soup. Freshly cooked dried beans lend an unbelievable creaminess that seeps out into the dark broth, giving it a beautiful thick and glossy consistency, while bacon adds a smoky quality. Puree leftovers into black bean dip, or strain the beans from the liquid and eat them over rice sprinkled with a little sugar and some fried plantains on the side.

1. Bring a large pot of water to a boil. Add the beans and cook for 3 minutes. Turn off the heat, cover, and let the beans soak for 1 hour.

2. Drain the beans through a sieve, rinse out the pot, and then return the beans to the pot along with the chicken stock. Bring to a boil, reduce the heat to low, cover, and gently simmer for 1 hour.

3. Meanwhile, place the bacon in a large skillet over medium-high heat. Cook, stirring occasionally, until the bacon is just starting to get crispy, 3 to 5 minutes. Reduce the heat to low and stir in the bell peppers, sofrito, garlic, and cumin. Once the peppers start to soften, after about 2 minutes, scrape the sofrito mixture into the pot with the beans. Add the bay leaves, cover, and cook, stirring occasionally, until the beans are tender, about 1 hour longer. Remove and discard the bay leaves. Divide the soup among six bowls and serve.

CREAMY ROASTED CORN SOUP

Serves 6

4 ears of corn, husked, kernels sliced off the cobs

2 tablespoons extra-virgin olive oil

2 teaspoons kosher salt

2 teaspoons freshly ground black pepper

1 cup Basic Sofrito (page 202)

1 garlic clove, roughly chopped

2 yellow summer squash, trimmed and roughly chopped

2 zucchini, trimmed and roughly chopped

5 cups Chicken Stock (page 211) or store-bought chicken broth

1/4 cup plus 1 tablespoon finely chopped fresh cilantro

1/4 cup heavy cream (optional)

We have been eating corn in South America for millennia. It is ground into flour to make arepas, pupusas, tamales, and tortillas; of course it's also used in its pure form in soups and stews like this one, which has a wonderfully roasty-nutty flavor thanks to oven toasting the corn and caramelizing its sugars before it goes into the soup. Enriching the sofrito with summer squash gives this soup an autumnal feel.

1. Preheat the oven to 400°F.

2. Place the corn kernels on a rimmed baking sheet and spread them out into an even layer. Drizzle with 2 tablespoons of the olive oil and then sprinkle with 1 teaspoon of the salt and 1 teaspoon of the pepper. Toss with your hands to evenly season the corn. Roast until lightly golden brown, about 20 minutes.

3. Meanwhile, heat the sofrito in a large soup pot over medium-high heat. Stir in the garlic, yellow squash, and zucchini, increase the heat to high, and cook, stirring often, until the squash softens, about 10 minutes.

4. Pour in the chicken stock and then stir in the 1/4 cup cilantro and 1 cup of the roasted corn. Bring to a simmer and cook until the soup is slightly reduced, about 5 minutes. Turn off the heat and set aside the soup to cool for about 10 minutes.

5. Use a ladle to transfer about one-third of the soup to a blender jar. Place the lid on the jar and pulse a few times to release the heat from the soup, then puree until smooth. Transfer the pureed soup to a clean pot. Repeat with another third of the soup. Before pureeing the last third, add the remaining 1 teaspoon salt and 1 teaspoon pepper, and the heavy cream, if using.

continued

6. Bring the soup to a boil in the pot and turn off the heat. Stir in the remaining roasted corn and divide the soup among six bowls. Divide the remaining 1 tablespoon cilantro among the bowls and serve immediately.

HUEVOS PERICOS

8 large eggs

3 tablespoons milk

1 teaspoon kosher salt

2 tablespoons vegetable oil

½ small yellow onion, finely chopped

1 small tomato, cored and finely chopped

¼ cup shredded cheddar cheese

2 scallions, white and light green parts only, finely chopped

¼ cup finely chopped fresh cilantro

½ cup shredded queso fresco

When we were kids, my brother and I proudly served this egg scramble to our mom on Mother's Day, and I've made it for breakfast or dinner at least a thousand times since. The eggs first get scrambled with onions and tomatoes, and then lots of cilantro and scallions are folded in. Though untraditional, grated cheddar cheese gives the eggs an extra hit of richness. A generous handful of queso fresco sprinkled over the top just before serving adds a wonderful sharpness.

1. Whisk together the eggs, milk, and salt in a large bowl and set aside.

2. Heat the vegetable oil in a large nonstick skillet over medium heat. Add the onions and tomatoes and cook, stirring often, until the onions are translucent and the tomatoes have released their juices, about 5 minutes.

3. Pour the egg mixture over the vegetables and, stirring constantly with a wooden spoon, scramble the eggs until they're cooked through, 3 to 4 minutes. Add the cheddar cheese and continue to stir until it is melted. Turn off the heat and stir in the scallions and cilantro. Divide the eggs among four plates, sprinkle with queso fresco, and serve.

CREMITA DI APIO

12 cups Chicken Stock (page 211) or store-bought chicken broth

1 pound boneless beef shanks or stew meat, cut into 1-inch pieces

2 pounds celeriac, peeled and cut into 1-inch pieces

2 carrots, roughly chopped

2 celery stalks, roughly chopped

1 large yellow onion, roughly chopped

1¼ cups whole cilantro leaves

1 cup Basic Sofrito (page 202)

1 tablespoon kosher salt

¼ cup heavy cream

1 tablespoon finely chopped fresh flat-leaf parsley

1 tablespoon finely chopped fresh thyme

In Venezuela, when you want to cook something special for a family gathering, you make a beautiful and elegant cream of celeriac soup. Celeriac, also called celery root, has a gentle flavor, somewhere between parsnips and celery—it manages to be delicate and hearty all at once. Serve with a loaf of crusty bread on the side.

1. Bring the chicken stock, beef, celeriac, carrots, celery, onions, and 1 cup of the whole cilantro leaves to a boil in a large pot over high heat. Cook for 5 minutes and then reduce the heat to medium-low. Continue to cook until the meat is tender and the vegetables are soft, about 15 minutes.

2. Stir in the sofrito and salt, cook for 1 minute, and then turn off the heat. Let the soup cool for 20 minutes.

3. Stir in the heavy cream, parsley, and thyme. Ladle one-third of the soup into a blender jar and blend until very smooth and airy, about 3 minutes. Pour the puree into a clean soup pot and repeat with the remaining soup in two additions. Divide the soup among six bowls, finish with some cilantro, and serve immediately.

AREPAS STUFFED *with* REINA PEPIADA

Makes 16 stuffed arepas

2 cups cooked and shredded chicken (about ¹/₂ rotisserie chicken)

1 large yellow onion, finely diced

³/₄ cup light mayonnaise

2 tablespoons of fresh lemon juice

¹/₂ cup finely chopped fresh cilantro
   Kosher salt and freshly ground black pepper

1 Hass avocado, halved, pitted, peeled, and finely diced

16 Venezuelan arepas (page 30), freshly made

Shredded chicken mixed with avocado and a touch of mayonnaise is called *reina pepiada;* in South America it is a popular staple for stuffing arepas and makes a great anytime meal. Use leftover baked chicken, a rotisserie chicken, or even chicken from Chicken Stock (see page 211). The avocado lends a creamy and satisfying texture. If you don't have time to make arepas, roll the filling in flat-bread, stuff it into pita, or pile it on top of your favorite sandwich bread.

1. Place the chicken in a large bowl. Add the onions, mayonnaise, lemon juice, and cilantro and salt and pepper to taste and stir to combine. Gently stir in the avocado, taste, and adjust the seasonings as needed.

2. Slice a slit into the top edge of each arepa and gently wiggle a paring knife into the arepa, creating a pocket. Divide the chicken salad among the arepas and serve.

NUEVO ARROZ CON POLLO

Serves 6

1 large yellow onion, finely chopped

5 tablespoons extra-virgin olive oil, plus 2 tablespoons if needed

1 tablespoon Worcestershire sauce

2 teaspoons kosher salt

1 teaspoon freshly ground black pepper

15 garlic cloves, very finely minced

One 3^1/$_2$- to 4-pound chicken, cut into 8 pieces, skin removed

1 cup fresh corn kernels (from about 1 ear)

3 celery stalks, sliced crosswise into ^{1}/$_2$-inch-thick pieces

2 tablespoons tomato paste

2 large Yukon gold potatoes, peeled and cut into ^{1}/$_2$-inch cubes

4 large carrots, chopped

2 cups long-grain brown rice

2^1/$_2$ cups Chicken Stock (page 211) or store-bought chicken broth

2 cups ale or lager-style beer

2 cups fresh cilantro leaves

^{1}/$_2$ cup thinly sliced roasted red pepper strips

^{1}/$_2$ cup frozen peas

3 scallions, light green parts only, thinly sliced

I have vivid memories from when I was a little girl watching my mother and grandmother cutting up a chicken to make arroz con pollo and rubbing the chicken with lemon juice to give it an amazing, citrusy head start before it even hit the pan. Here, I take the flavor one step further, marinating the chicken with onions, garlic, and Worcestershire sauce to really pump it up from within. Then the dish is cooked in a style similar to making paella—browning the chicken, vegetables, and tomato paste in a pot to bring out their sweetness before adding brown rice, chicken stock, and beer to cook. The dish steams together and becomes a deeper, more robust-tasting version of the classic.

1. Take about one-quarter of the chopped onions and finely chop so you have 2 tablespoons of finely minced onions (set the remaining onions aside for later). Place 2 tablespoons of the olive oil, the Worcestershire sauce, salt, and black pepper in a gallon-size resealable plastic bag. Add the very finely chopped onions and three-quarters of the garlic, seal the bag, and then vigorously shake to combine. Add the chicken to the bag, toss to coat in the marinade, seal the bag, and refrigerate for at least 1 hour or overnight.

2. Heat the remaining 3 tablespoons olive oil in a large heavy-bottomed pot or Dutch oven over high heat. Remove the chicken from the marinade and add it to the pan (discard the marinade). Cook until the chicken is golden brown, 6 to 8 minutes on each side. Transfer the chicken to a paper towel–lined plate or rimmed baking sheet and set aside.

3. Add the reserved onions and up to 2 more tablespoons olive oil to the pan if needed and cook for 1 minute. Stir in the corn, celery, remaining garlic, and tomato paste and cook until the garlic is fragrant, about 1 minute. Add the potatoes and carrots and cook, stirring often, until they are well coated with the tomato paste and the bottom of the pan gets sticky, about 3 minutes.

4. Stir the rice into the vegetables and then return the chicken to the pan. Pour in the chicken stock and beer, stir in the cilantro, and bring the liquid to a boil. Reduce the heat to medium-high and simmer the mixture until slightly reduced, about 5 minutes. Cover the pan, reduce the heat to low, and cook until the rice is cooked through, about 35 minutes.

5. Uncover the pan and carefully lay the red pepper strips over the top. Sprinkle the peas in an even layer over the peppers, re-cover the pan, and cook for 1 hour longer. Uncover, sprinkle the scallions over the top, and serve.

YUCCA *with* GARLIC-HERB MOJITO

Serves 6

1½ pounds yucca, peeled, halved lengthwise, and sliced crosswise into 1-inch lengths

¼ cup extra-virgin olive oil

1 tablespoon unsalted butter

6 garlic cloves, very finely minced

2 tablespoons finely chopped fresh cilantro

1 tablespoon finely chopped fresh thyme

1 tablespoon finely chopped fresh flat-leaf parsley

½ lemon

1 teaspoon kosher salt

½ teaspoon freshly ground black pepper

While Americans know a mojito as a sweet rum and mint drink from Brazil, in other parts of South America a mojito is the name of a wonderfully pungent and delicious vinaigrette made from garlic, herbs, and citrus. It's often served alongside fried yucca or *tostones* (fried green plantain cakes), but here, it's paired with delicate-textured and nutty-tasting blanched yucca. This recipe calls for lemon juice and a combination of cilantro, thyme, and parsley in the mojito, but feel free to adapt the recipe to suit whatever you have in the house—from blood oranges or champagne vinegar to basil, mint, or chives. This side dish is excellent alongside barbecued meat or roasted chicken.

1. Fill a large soup pot or stockpot three-quarters full with water. Add the yucca and bring to a boil over high heat. Reduce the heat to medium-low and simmer until the yucca is tender, 15 to 20 minutes. Drain through a colander, transfer the yucca to a shallow platter, and set aside.

2. Heat the olive oil with the butter in a small skillet over medium-high heat. Once the butter is melted, turn off the heat and add the garlic, cilantro, thyme, and parsley, swirling it in the melted butter mixture to temper the garlic and gently soften the herbs. Pour the mojito over the yucca and then squeeze the lemon over the top. Sprinkle the yucca with the salt and pepper and serve.

BLACK LENTIL *and* BELL PEPPER SALAD
with FRESH MINT

Serves 4

1 cup black beluga lentils

2 teaspoons kosher salt

¼ green bell pepper, finely chopped

¼ red bell pepper, finely chopped

¼ yellow bell pepper, finely chopped

½ small red onion, finely chopped

2 tablespoons extra-virgin olive oil

1 tablespoon fresh lemon juice

½ teaspoon freshly ground black pepper

¼ cup finely chopped fresh cilantro

1½ teaspoons finely chopped fresh mint

Each year on December 31, I eat a bowl of lentils at midnight for good luck and abundance in the new year. Lentils play a big role in Venezuelans' diets, and we often eat them simply boiled with a bowl of white rice on the side. In this side dish, I keep to that principle of simplicity but add all kinds of vibrant colors and flavors—like fresh mint, lemon juice, and cilantro (of course!)—to give the salad character. This is a lovely accompaniment to fish or meat or a great main course for a meat-free meal. You can make the lentils ahead and hold them for a few days in the refrigerator. Add in the rest of the ingredients before serving and enjoy the delicious results.

1. Place a bowl of ice water on the counter. Bring a large pot of water to a boil. Add the lentils and salt, return to a boil, reduce the heat to medium-low, and simmer until the lentils are tender, about 25 minutes. Strain through a fine-mesh sieve and then plunge the lentils (still in the sieve) into the ice water to chill them. Remove, shake off the extra water, and repeat if necessary until the lentils are completely cooled. Turn the lentils out into a large bowl. Add the bell peppers and onions to the lentils and stir to combine.

2. Whisk together the olive oil, lemon juice, and black pepper in a small bowl. Stir in the cilantro and mint and then scrape the mixture over the lentils. Stir to combine and serve immediately or refrigerate for up to 4 days. The salad can be served cold or at room temperature.

ALL STARS:
RESTAURANT BEST SELLERS AT HOME

While I'm most at home in the kitchen of my house, I am a restaurant line cook at heart. I love being in the zone—the pressure, the chaos, the cooking. When I opened my first restaurant, a little eight-table spot in Miami's Design District, I had a limited budget, no investors, and a lot of heart and ambition. I remember going to the local businesses one by one, literally knocking on their doors and personally inviting people to come to eat at my restaurant.

After six months of long hours over the stove, I could count on a queue of people lined up out the door, waiting for a table. Soon I expanded from eight to fourteen tables, and then to a new, larger space. But when I started spending more time in a television studio than in my kitchen, taping "El Arte del Buen Gusto," "Cocine," and "Sazon con Lorena Garcia," rather than hiring someone to take over, I decided to step away from the restaurant business. Now that Lorena Garcia Cocina, my fast, casual, and healthy airport restaurant is up and running, I am excited to have found a happy medium.

The dishes in this chapter represent my signatures, happy creations like creamy savory-sweet plantain soup, succulent filet mignon spiked with a passion fruit demi-glaze and blue cheese, and incredibly decadent yet homey braised short ribs in a bay leaf and currant sauce. Each dish is unique, emphasizing big flavors with a Latin spin, and all are simple enough for a weeknight meal or a weekend entertaining with friends.

RISOTTO *with* CARAMELIZED WALNUTS *and* FRESH APRICOTS

Serves 6

continued

FOR THE WALNUTS

- ¼ cup Chicken Stock (page 211) or store-bought chicken broth
- 1 tablespoon fresh lemon juice
- 3 tablespoons sugar
- ½ cup walnut halves

FOR THE RISOTTO

- 2 tablespoons unsalted butter
- 1 cup finely chopped fresh apricots
- 1½ tablespoons sugar
- 3 cups Chicken Stock (page 211) or store-bought chicken broth
- 1 tablespoon extra-virgin olive oil
- 1 shallot, very finely chopped
- 6 garlic cloves, very finely minced
- 1 cup Arborio rice
- ½ cup dry white wine (such as pinot grigio)
- ½ cup grated Parmigiano-Reggiano cheese
- 6 small fresh basil leaves

With waves of sweetness, crunchiness, and a fruit-cheese finish, this rich risotto is my version of a cheese plate. It's very decadent and best shared among a few people, either as a small starter or as an hors d'oeuvre (try scooping a little onto spoons and lining them up on a tray). Make this dish in the summer, when fresh apricots are at their best. For a more substantial meal, add some thinly sliced or shredded grilled or sautéed chicken breasts.

1. Line a plate with parchment or wax paper and set aside.

2. To caramelize the walnuts, pour the chicken stock into a small skillet. Add the lemon juice, sugar, and walnuts and bring to a boil over high heat. Cook, stirring often, until the liquid is evaporated and the walnuts are caramelized and sticky, 3 to 4 minutes. Immediately scrape the walnuts onto the paper-lined plate. Set aside to cool completely, about 20 minutes.

3. To make the risotto, melt the butter in a medium skillet over medium heat. Add the apricots and sugar and cook, stirring occasionally, until the apricots are golden brown, about five minutes. Set aside.

4. Pour the chicken stock into a medium saucepan and heat over medium heat. Once the broth is warmed through, reduce the heat to low and cover. Heat the olive oil in a large heavy-bottomed pot over medium-high heat. Add the shallots, garlic, rice, and white wine and cook, stirring often, until the liquid is evaporated, about 3 minutes.

5. Add 1 cup warmed chicken stock to the rice mixture, stirring constantly, until the broth is completely absorbed by the rice, 3 to 5 minutes. Repeat two times, stirring the rice in be-

continued

tween additions and letting it absorb all the broth before adding the next cup. At this point, the rice should be tender. Turn off the heat and stir in the Parmigiano-Reggiano cheese.

6. Divide the risotto among six plates. Top it with 1 tablespoon of the apricots and a few walnuts. Stack the basil leaves and roll them into a cylinder, then thinly slice them crosswise and sprinkle over the risotto.

Sabes Qué?

Eating fruit when it's at its seasonal peak is the best time to experience its fullest, sweetest flavors. When apricots are not in season this risotto is just as delicious with other fruits like apples, pears, or even butternut squash.

TROPICAL CRAB CAKES

Makes 8 crab cakes

3 tablespoons extra-virgin olive oil

2 turkey bacon strips, chopped into small pieces

1 cup Basic Sofrito (page 202)

3/4 cup fresh corn kernels (from 1 ear)

1 tablespoon finely chopped fresh cilantro

1/2 teaspoon ground cumin

1/2 teaspoon sweet paprika

2 tablespoons dry white wine (such as sauvignon blanc)

1 cup fresh lump crabmeat (about 1/2 pound)

1/3 cup light mayonnaise

1 tablespoon Dijon mustard

1 tablespoon fresh lemon juice

1/4 cup dried unseasoned bread crumbs

1 teaspoon kosher salt

1/2 teaspoon freshly ground black pepper

1 cup buttermilk

1 large egg

2 cups panko bread crumbs

1/4 cup Tropical Passion Fruit Vinaigrette (page 75)

This favorite appetizer gets a light and Latin makeover with some key ingredients: a cooked sofrito of tomatoes, onions, and peppers, and some browned turkey bacon. A vivacious and tangy passion fruit vinaigrette spikes the crab cake with an exotic and bright taste that makes more sense than pairing it with a heavy mayonnaise-based dipping sauce. To keep the flavor fresh, start the crab cakes off in a skillet and then move them to the oven, where they'll finish cooking and crisping up.

1. Place 1 tablespoon of the olive oil and the turkey bacon in a large skillet over high heat until the bacon starts to render and brown, 2 to 3 minutes. Stir in the sofrito, corn, cilantro, cumin, and paprika. Pour in the white wine, bring to a simmer, and cook until the wine is slightly reduced, about 2 minutes. Remove from the heat, transfer to a large bowl, and set aside for 10 minutes to cool.

2. Add the crabmeat to the sofrito-bacon base and gently toss, trying not to break up the larger pieces of crabmeat.

3. Whisk together the mayonnaise, mustard, and lemon juice in a small bowl and then add it into the crab mixture, gently stirring to combine. Stir in the unseasoned bread crumbs, salt, and pepper.

4. Scoop out a heaping 1/4 cup of the crab mixture, lightly shape it into a ball (don't pack it tightly), and then slightly flatten. Set the crab cake aside and repeat with the remaining crab mixture.

5. Beat together the buttermilk and egg in a medium bowl. Place the panko bread crumbs in a shallow dish. Dip both sides of the crab cake into the buttermilk mixture and then

continued

press the crab cake into the panko, evenly coating both sides. Place the breaded crab cake on a large plate and repeat with the remaining crab cakes. Cover the plate with plastic wrap and refrigerate the crab cakes for at least 20 minutes (or up to 1 day).

6. Preheat the oven to 400°F.

7. Heat the remaining 2 tablespoons olive oil in a large non-stick skillet over medium-high heat. Add the crab cakes and cook until browned, about 4 minutes. Flip over the crab cakes and brown the other sides, about 4 minutes longer. Turn off the heat and transfer the crab cakes to a rimmed baking sheet.

8. Bake the crab cakes until they're golden brown and crisp, 20 to 25 minutes. Serve them warm with a drizzle of the passion fruit vinaigrette.

CREAMY PLANTAIN MADUROS SOUP

Serves 6

nonstick vegetable cooking spray

3 ripe plantains, peeled and cut into
1 1/2-inch pieces

2 tablespoons extra-virgin olive oil

1 small yellow onion, roughly chopped

1 carrot, roughly chopped

1 celery stalk, roughly chopped

2 small yellow summer squash,
trimmed and thinly sliced

3 cups Chicken Stock (page 211) or
store-bought chicken broth

1 tablespoon kosher salt, plus more to
taste

1 teaspoon freshly ground black pepper,
plus more to taste

2 cups low-fat milk

1/4 cup fresh cilantro leaves

store-bought plantain chips (optional)

Sweet Plantains Maduros (page 206) is a traditional South American side dish of ripe plantains sliced into bite-size pieces and panfried until golden brown, honey sweet, and creamy tender. Rich with just a hint of caramel-y sweetness, I tap the flavor of fried maduros in this signature creamy (but cream-less) soup. I first served it at my Miami restaurant Food Café. Plantains look like large bananas. When they are underripe, they are green and have a savory potatolike texture and flavor that hints of banana. As they ripen, they become very yellow, and then start to blacken. This is how you know they are sweet and sticky under the thick peel.

1. Preheat the oven to 350°F. Line a rimmed baking sheet with aluminum foil and lightly grease it using nonstick vegetable cooking spray.

2. Place the plantains on the aluminum foil. Bake until golden brown, about 40 minutes. Remove from the oven and set aside to cool.

3. Heat the olive oil in a large pot over medium heat. Add the onions, carrots, and celery and cook, stirring once or twice, until they're beginning to soften, about 2 minutes. Stir in the squash and cook until tender, stirring occasionally, about 3 minutes longer. Pour in the chicken stock and add the salt and pepper. Increase the heat to high, bring the broth to a boil, reduce the heat to medium-low, and gently simmer until all of the vegetables are very soft, about 10 minutes. Turn off the heat and let the soup cool for 10 minutes.

4. Place one-half of the cooked plantains into a blender jar. Use a slotted spoon to add about one-half of the squash mix-

continued

ture to the blender. Add one-half of the broth and 1 cup of the milk. Cover the blender and then pulse the ingredients together to release some of the heat. Puree until completely smooth, and then pour the puree into a clean pot. Repeat with the remaining plantains, squash mixture, broth, and milk.

5. Bring the soup to a boil over medium-high heat, reduce the heat to low, cover the pot, and simmer for 5 minutes. Season with salt and pepper and divide the soup among six bowls. Garnish with the cilantro and plantain chips, if using, and serve immediately.

Sabes Qué?

This soup is a great way to use up lots of leftover plantain maduros. If you don't happen to have enough remaining from dinner the night before, boost your supply with some maduros ordered from a South American restaurant. Skip the first two steps of the recipe and start with sautéing the onions, carrots, and celery in olive oil. Add the cooked plantains to the blender following the recipe instructions.

BUTTERNUT SQUASH, COCONUT, *and* LEMONGRASS SOUP

Serves 8

1 large butternut squash, peeled, halved, seeded, and chopped into 1-inch pieces

½ teaspoon kosher salt

Pinch of freshly ground black pepper

2 tablespoons extra-virgin olive oil

1 tablespoon unsalted butter

2 large yellow onions, chopped into 1-inch pieces

2 carrots, sliced crosswise into 1-inch lengths

2 celery stalks, sliced crosswise into 1-inch lengths

2 leeks, white and light green parts only, halved lengthwise and thinly sliced crosswise

2 lemongrass stalks, trimmed

1 large zucchini, trimmed, halved lengthwise and sliced crosswise into 1-inch lengths

2 bay leaves

1 cup dry white wine (such as pinot grigio)

5 cups Chicken Stock (page 211) or store-bought chicken or vegetable broth

One 15-ounce can light coconut milk

1 bunch fresh cilantro, roughly chopped

1 tablespoon toasted, shredded coconut (optional)

Whipping this soup in the blender adds body and makes the naturally creamy butternut squash puree even lighter. For an extra hit of coconut flavor, add ½ cup shaved unsweetened coconut to the blender along with the soup (strain the soup after pureeing for a super-smooth texture).

1. Preheat the oven to 400°F. Line a rimmed baking sheet with aluminum foil.

2. Place the butternut squash on the prepared baking sheet, season with the salt and pepper, and toss with 1 tablespoon of the olive oil. Roast until lightly caramelized and a paring knife easily slides into a piece of squash, about 1 hour. Remove the squash from the oven and set aside to cool.

3. Melt the butter with the remaining 1 tablespoon olive oil in a large pot over medium-high heat. Add the onions, carrots, celery, leeks, lemongrass, zucchini, bay leaves, and roasted squash and cook, stirring often, until the vegetables soften and turn golden brown around the edges, 8 to 10 minutes.

4. Pour in the white wine and bring it to a boil, stirring and scraping up any browned bits from the bottom of the pot. Once the wine is mostly evaporated, pour in the chicken stock and bring it to a boil. Reduce the heat to medium-low and cook until all the vegetables are soft, 10 to 12 minutes. Turn off the heat and discard the lemongrass and the bay leaves. Set the soup aside to cool for 20 minutes.

5. Transfer one-half of the vegetables and broth to a blender jar. Cover and pulse a few times to release the steam. Add one-half of the coconut milk and puree the mixture until it's

continued

completely smooth. Transfer the soup to a clean pot. Repeat with the remaining vegetables and broth, and coconut milk. Bring the soup back to a simmer over high heat, reduce the heat to medium-low, and simmer for 5 minutes. Turn off the heat. Divide the soup among eight bowls and serve sprinkled with cilantro and toasted coconut (if using).

Sabes Qué?

To make peeling the butternut squash easier, give it a go in the microwave. Halve the squash lengthwise, scrape out the seeds, and place the halves on a microwave-safe plate, cut side down. Cook in 1-minute increments until the squash is a little soft. Remove it from the microwave and once it's cool enough to handle, use a paring knife to peel away the skin. Then chop it with ease.

SESAME-BALSAMIC SASHIMI TUNA
with WASABI MAYO *and* BABY GREENS

Serves 4

FOR THE MAYO

3 tablespoons light mayonnaise

2 tablespoons wasabi paste

2 tablespoons rice vinegar

2 garlic cloves, very finely minced

FOR THE TUNA

3/4 cup black sesame seeds

3/4 cup white sesame seeds

Four 6-ounce sushi-grade tuna fillets

1 1/2 teaspoons vegetable oil

3 cups baby greens

3/4 cup Caramelized Walnuts (page 212)

3/4 cup Balsamic Vinaigrette (page 74)

Pinch of kosher salt

Pinch of freshly ground black pepper

1 cup bottled balsamic glaze

The grapy-vinegary flavor of the balsamic glaze that gets drizzled over the seared tuna before serving works with the nuttiness of the sesame seeds and the spiciness of the pungent wasabi mayo. The textures of this dish also hit all the right notes with the delicate and crisp sesame-coated tuna and the crunch of the caramelized walnuts in the salad. The wasabi mayo can be refrigerated for up to one week.

1. To make the wasabi mayo, whisk together the mayonnaise, wasabi paste, rice vinegar, garlic, and 1 tablespoon of water in a small bowl. Cover the bowl with plastic wrap and refrigerate (it can be made up to 1 week in advance).

2. To make the tuna, combine the black and white sesame seeds in a shallow bowl or pie plate. Place the tuna in the sesame seeds and gently press down so the sesame seeds stick to the fish and completely cover the surface. Repeat on the other side.

3. Heat the vegetable oil in a large skillet over high heat. Add the tuna to the pan and cook it on each side until the sesame seeds are toasted and fragrant, about 4 minutes total (you want to keep the tuna rare in the middle). Transfer the tuna to a cutting board and set aside to cool while you make the salad.

4. Place the greens in a medium bowl, add the walnuts, and toss with the vinaigrette, salt, and pepper.

5. Slice the tuna crosswise into 1/4-inch-thick pieces and fan them out on each plate. Top with some of the salad and then place a dollop of the wasabi mayo on the side of each plate. Drizzle with the balsamic glaze and serve.

CHILLED SHRIMP *and* PERUVIAN CORN SALAD

Serves 4

FOR THE SHRIMP

- 1 lemon, cut into wedges
- 16 jumbo shrimp (about 1 pound), peeled and deveined

FOR THE CORN SALAD

- 1 cup Peruvian corn or fresh or frozen (thawed) sweet corn
- ½ cup finely chopped jicama
- 1 medium jalapeño pepper, halved and finely chopped (seeded and deveined for less heat)
- 2 tablespoons finely chopped fresh cilantro
- 2 tablespoons finely chopped fresh mint
- 1 tablespoon extra-virgin olive oil

  zest of lime plus 1 tablespoon fresh lime juice
- ½ teaspoon kosher salt
- ½ teaspoon freshly ground black pepper

  Spicy Guasacaca Salsita (page 194)

There are more than fifty different varieties of corn grown in Peru. The kind known as Peruvian corn has large kernels with a nice crunchy texture. You can find it frozen in Latin markets or use fresh or frozen local sweet corn instead. *Guasacaca* is Venezuela's version of guacamole. Like guacamole, it is composed of avocados and includes jalapeños, onions, and garlic. It is served semichunky or can be pureed until smooth and used as a sauce.

1. Place a large bowl of ice water on the counter. Fill a medium saucepan with 2 cups of water. Add the lemon wedges and bring to a boil over high heat. Reduce the heat to a gentle simmer, set a steamer basket in the pan, and place the shrimp in the basket. Cover the pan and cook the shrimp until they are pink and opaque, about 3 minutes. Use tongs to transfer the shrimp to the ice water to stop the cooking process. Once the shrimp are completely cold, remove them from the ice water and place them in a medium bowl. Set aside.

2. Place the corn in a medium bowl and add the jicama, jalapeño, cilantro, and mint, stirring to combine. In a small bowl whisk together the oil, lime juice, salt, and black pepper and pour the dressing over the corn mixture. Stir to combine and set aside.

3. Place the guasacaca in the bowl of a food processor and puree until completely smooth, scraping the sides and bottom of the bowl as needed.

4. Divide the pureed guasacaca mixture amoung four plates, and using the back of a spoon, spread it out evenly. Top with ¼ cup of the corn salad, 4 shrimp, and a little of the lime zest. Serve immediately.

GREEN GODDESS COBB SALAD

Serves 4

⅓ cup plus 2 tablespoons light mayonnaise

¼ cup finely chopped fresh cilantro leaves

¼ cup grated Parmigiano-Reggiano cheese

2 teaspoons white vinegar

1½ teaspoons fresh lime juice

½ teaspoon Dijon mustard

½ small garlic clove

⅛ teaspoon kosher salt

Pinch freshly ground black pepper

4 cups baby greens

½ cup Caramelized Walnuts (page 212)

Instead of finishing the salad with strawberries, blackberries, or raspberries, finish it with more traditional Cobb salad toppings like chopped hard-boiled eggs, crumbled crisp-fried bacon, chopped tomatoes, and chopped avocados.

1. Place the mayonnaise, cilantro, Parmesan cheese, vinegar, lime juice, mustard, garlic, salt, pepper, and 1½ teaspoons of water in a blender jar. Cover and puree until completely smooth.

2. Gently toss the greens with the dressing in a large bowl. Divide the baby greens between four plates, mounding the greens in the center. Sprinkle 2 tablespoons of the walnuts around each serving of greens and serve.

The Perfect Vinaigrette for Any Salad

A homemade vinaigrette is simple, inexpensive, and quick to make, whether you're dressing salad greens, grilled vegetables, seafood, or meat. These are the ones I make the most often. I always keep one or two in the fridge to finish up quick last-minute meals. They can all be refrigerated in a covered container for up to three days.

BALSAMIC VINAIGRETTE

Makes about 1½ cup

½ cup balsamic vinegar
6 tablespoons honey
1 tablespoon Dijon mustard
½ teaspoon kosher salt
¼ teaspoon freshly ground black pepper
3 tablespoons extra-virgin olive oil

Place the balsamic vinegar, honey, mustard, salt, and pepper in a blender jar, cover, and blend on high speed. Stop the blender, remove the insert from the blender lid, and mix on medium speed while drizzling in the olive oil. Add ¼ cup of water and blend to combine. Pour the vinaigrette into an airtight container or glass jar and refrigerate. Shake well before using.

TANGY CITRUS VINAIGRETTE

Makes about 2 cups

2 tablespoons Dijon mustard
6 tablespoons agave syrup
6 tablespoons fresh lemon juice (from 2 lemons)
6 tablespoons fresh orange juice (from 1½ oranges)
6 tablespoons extra-virgin olive oil
1 tablespoon kosher salt
1 tablespoon freshly ground black pepper

Whisk together the mustard, agave syrup, lemon juice, and orange juice in a medium bowl. While whisking, slowly drizzle in the olive oil and then whisk in the salt and pepper. Pour the vinaigrette into an airtight container or glass jar and refrigerate. Shake well before using.

TROPICAL PASSION FRUIT VINAIGRETTE

Makes about 2 cups

1 cup mango juice

1 cup fresh orange juice

1 cup passion fruit juice

2 teaspoons whole pink peppercorns

2 tablespoons agave syrup

2 tablespoons Dijon mustard

3 tablespoons champagne vinegar

6 tablespoons extra-virgin olive oil

2 teaspoons kosher salt

1. Pour the mango juice, orange juice, and passion fruit juice into a medium saucepan. Add the peppercorns and bring to a simmer over medium heat. Reduce the heat to medium-low and simmer gently until the liquid reduces by half, 20 to 25 minutes. Set aside to cool to room temperature.

2. Whisk the agave syrup and mustard into the juice mixture and then whisk in the vinegar. While whisking, slowly drizzle in the olive oil and then whisk in the salt. Pour the vinaigrette into an airtight container or glass jar and refrigerate. Shake well before using.

BLOOD ORANGE VINAIGRETTE

Makes about 2 cups

1 cup blood orange juice (from 2 blood oranges)

2 tablespoons fresh lemon juice

2 tablespoons rice vinegar

1 small shallot, very finely chopped

2 teaspoons sugar

1/2 cup extra-virgin olive oil

1 teaspoon kosher salt

1/2 teaspoon freshly ground black pepper

Whisk together the blood orange juice, lemon juice, and rice vinegar in a medium bowl. Whisk in the shallots and sugar until the sugar is dissolved. While whisking, slowly drizzle in the olive oil and then whisk in the salt and pepper. Pour the vinaigrette into an airtight container or glass jar and refrigerate. Shake well before using.

TRUFFLED SALMON OVER
ROASTED PLANTAINS

Serves 4

FOR THE TRUFFLE BUTTER

- 4 tablespoons (1/2 stick) unsalted butter, at room temperature
- 2 tablespoons black truffle oil
- 1 tablespoon sliced fresh or jarred black truffles

FOR THE PLANTAINS

- 1 ripe, completely blackened plantain, peeled and thinly sliced on the diagonal
- 2 tablespoons extra-virgin olive oil
- 1/2 teaspoon kosher salt

  Pinch of freshly ground black pepper

FOR THE SALMON

- Four 6-ounce salmon fillets
- 1 teaspoon kosher salt
- 1/2 teaspoon freshly ground black pepper
- 1/2 teaspoon vegetable oil
- 1/2 cup dry white wine (such as pinot grigio)
- 1/2 cup Chicken Stock (page 211) or store-bought chicken broth

One of my favorite ways to make a simple food elegant is with a compound butter—a softened butter mixed with aromatics, spices, citrus zest, herbs, or, as in this case, ultraindulgent truffles. For a rich flavor boost, add a little pat to farm-fresh roasted vegetables, charred grilled fish, a simple piece of pan-seared chicken, pasta, or even to finish risotto or a sauce. Keep several different varieties in the fridge or freezer (it keeps fresh for up to five days in the refrigerator and three months in the freezer) to give an otherwise straightforward dish—like this pan-seared salmon with oven-roasted plantain slices—an amazing, bright taste.

1. To make the truffle butter, place the butter, truffle oil, and black truffles in the bowl of a food processor and blend until the truffles are completely incorporated. Use a rubber spatula to scrape the mixture out onto the lower half of a long sheet of plastic wrap. Fold the top portion of the plastic wrap over the butter and gently roll and shape it into a 1 1/2-inch-wide log. Twist the ends of the plastic to seal. Freeze or refrigerate the butter until it is hard, about 2 hours. (The butter can be refrigerated up to 5 days or frozen up to 3 months.)

2. To make the plantain slices, preheat the oven to 350°F and line a rimmed baking sheet with parchment paper. Place the plantain slices on the prepared baking sheet and drizzle them with the olive oil. Sprinkle with the salt and pepper. Cook until the plantains are dark brown, about 20 minutes.

3. Meanwhile, to make the salmon, season the fish with the salt and pepper. Heat a large nonstick skillet over high heat. Add the vegetable oil and place the salmon flesh side down in

continued

the pan. Cook without moving until the underside is golden brown, 2 to 3 minutes. Use a spatula to flip over the salmon to cook the other side until it is golden brown, another 2 to 3 minutes. Pour in the white wine and chicken stock and cook until the sauce is reduced by half and the salmon is cooked through, 5 to 7 minutes longer.

4. Slice the log of truffle butter into 4 pieces. Divide the plantains among four plates. Place a piece of salmon on top of the plantains and a pad of truffle butter on each piece of fish (the butter should melt right over the salmon). Divide the sauce from the pan among the plates and serve.

MASHED PURPLE POTATOES
with ROASTED GARLIC

Serves 6

- 1 large garlic head, top third sliced off to expose the garlic cloves
- 1 tablespoon extra-virgin olive oil
- 2½ teaspoons kosher salt, plus more to taste
- 1 pound Peruvian purple or Yukon Gold potatoes, halved
- ¾ cup milk
- 3 tablespoons unsalted butter
- 2 teaspoons freshly ground black pepper, plus more to taste

One of the best ways to serve these Peruvian purple poatoes is mashed because they have a natural creaminess and buttery flavor. A head of oven-roasted garlic adds a soft, nutty flavor. I prefer mashed potatoes that have a bit of texture, but if you prefer a smooth mash, then finish the potatoes using a whisk instead of a fork.

1. Preheat the oven to 350°F.

2. Place the garlic in the center of a 6-inch square of aluminum foil, exposed cloves face up. Drizzle with olive oil, sprinkle with ½ teaspoon of the salt, and bring the corners of the foil up to the top of the head, gathering them together to seal the packet. Place the garlic on a baking sheet and roast until very soft, 35 to 40 minutes. Set the garlic aside to cool.

3. While the garlic cools, place the halved potatoes and ½ teaspoon of the salt in a large pot and cover with cold water. Bring the potatoes to a boil over high heat and cook them until tender, 15 to 20 minutes. Use a slotted spoon to transfer the potatoes to a rimmed baking sheet and set aside.

4. Pour the milk into a small saucepan. Add the butter, the remaining 1½ teaspoons salt, and the pepper and warm gently over medium heat, stirring often, until the butter is melted.

5. Transfer the potatoes to a large bowl. Squeeze the bottom of the head of roasted garlic to coax out the cloves, letting them fall into the bowl with the potatoes. Add a little bit of the milk mixture and use a fork to begin to mash everything together, drizzling in more liquid a little at a time until the potatoes are mashed to desired consistency. Taste and adjust the seasoning if needed.

GRILLED SEA BASS *with* PISTACHIO CRUST *and* TROPICAL PASSION FRUIT VINAIGRETTE

Serves 4

FOR THE PISTACHIO BUTTER

- 1 cup shelled pistachio nuts
- 8 tablespoons (1 stick) unsalted butter, cut into ¹/₂-inch cubes
- 1 cup fresh flat-leaf parsley leaves
- ¹/₂ cup fresh cilantro leaves
- ¹/₄ cup panko bread crumbs

FOR THE SEA BASS

- Four 4-ounce sea bass fillets
- 1¹/₂ teaspoons extra-virgin olive oil
- 1 tablespoon kosher salt
- 1¹/₂ teaspoons freshly ground black pepper
- 4 cups baby greens (such as arugula or spinach)
- 1¹/₂ cups Tropical Passion Fruit Vinaigrette (page 75)

Sea bass is rich, flaky, and quite elegant. Here it's paired with the richness of pistachios. As the pistachios and butter melt over the fillet, the bits of pistachio stick to the fish, creating a crustlike texture and a stunning presentation. To cut through all of these rich flavors, the fish is finished with a tropical passion fruit vinaigrette. It's unexpected and totally fantastic. Make extra pistachio butter for tossing with cheese ravioli or fresh pasta.

1. Place the pistachios in the bowl of a food processor for five 1-second pulses to roughly chop them. Add the butter, parsley, cilantro, and panko. Process the mixture until the butter is well combined and the pistachios are finely ground, 30 to 45 seconds. Use a rubber spatula to scrape the mixture out onto the lower half of a long piece of plastic wrap. Fold the top portion of the plastic wrap over the butter, and gently roll and shape it into a 1¹/₂-inch-wide log. Twist the ends of the plastic to seal. Refrigerate for at least 2 hours or up to 5 days (or freeze for up to 3 months).

2. Prepare a hot charcoal or gas grill. (If using a charcoal grill, follow the manufacturers' instructions to make a two-level fire, with one side of the grill at high heat and the other side at medium-low heat; if using a gas grill, adjust the burners so one side is at high heat and the other is at medium-low heat.)

3. To make the sea bass, set the fish on a rimmed baking sheet or on a large plate and drizzle with the olive oil. Sprinkle with the salt and pepper. Slice the chilled pistachio butter into 4 pieces.

continued

4. Grill the sea bass fillets flesh side down until they have grill marks, about 5 minutes. Carefully turn over the fillets and reduce the heat to medium (if using a charcoal grill, flip over the fillets onto the cooler side). Place a piece of the pistachio butter on top of each fillet, cover the grill, and continue to cook the fillets until they flake easily and are opaque all the way through, about 5 minutes longer, depending on how thick they are. Remove them from the grill and set aside.

5. Divide the baby greens among four plates. Place a piece of sea bass on top of the greens, drizzle with the passion fruit vinaigrette, and serve.

CARAMELIZED APPLE *and* WALNUT–STUFFED
PORK LOIN *with* VANILLA MANGO SAUCE

Serves 6

FOR THE PORK LOIN

- 2 tablespoons unsalted butter
- 1 Granny Smith apple, halved, cored, and finely chopped
- ¼ cup sugar
  One 2-pound center-cut pork loin
- 1 tablespoon kosher salt, plus more to taste
- 1½ teaspoons freshly ground black pepper, plus more to taste
- ½ cup finely chopped walnuts
- 2 tablespoons extra-virgin olive oil
- 1 cup dry white wine (such as pinot grigio)

FOR THE SAUCE

- 1½ cups fresh orange juice
- ¼ cup mango juice
- ¼ cup agave syrup
- 1 vanilla bean, halved lengthwise, seeds scraped away and reserved
- 2 tablespoons unsalted butter
- 1 teaspoon kosher salt

What inspires my cooking most is traveling to other places and getting a taste for the local cuisine. When I came home from a trip to Maui, for example, I couldn't get the taste memory of soft and floral vanilla combined with tropical fruit out of my head! So I re-created the flavor of Hawaii in an apple and walnut–stuffed pork loin that gets finished with an almost electric tropical mango sauce. This is a great make-ahead recipe. You can stuff the roast ahead of time and then pop it into the oven when your guests arrive. For maximum impact, bring it out on a large platter and carve it tableside.

1. To make the pork loin, melt the butter in a large skillet over high heat. Add the apples and sprinkle with the sugar, stirring to evenly coat the apples. Cook, stirring often, until the apples are golden brown and soft, about 5 minutes. Turn off the heat and set aside to cool.

2. Preheat the oven to 350°F.

3. Place the pork loin on a cutting board. Make a lengthwise end-to-end incision ½ inch from the bottom of the pork loin. Continue to slice through the pork loin, unraveling the loin as you go, until the pork loin lies flat on the cutting board in one sheet. Use a meat pounder to gently pound the pork to an even ½-inch thickness.

4. Season the top of the pork with the salt and pepper. Spread the cooled caramelized apples in an even layer over the surface of the pork and then sprinkle the walnuts over the apples. Roll up the loin into a tight log using butcher's twine to tie the loin shut at 2-inch intervals. Season the surface of the loin with salt and pepper.

continued

5. Heat the olive oil in a large ovenproof skillet over high heat. Add the pork loin and cook until golden brown on all sides, about 2 minutes per side. Pour in the white wine and, using a wooden spoon, scrape up any browned bits from the bottom of the pan. Transfer the pan to the oven and cook until a digital thermometer inserted into the center of the loin reads 160°F, about 1 hour. Remove the pork loin from the oven, tent with aluminum foil, and set aside to rest for 15 minutes.

6. While the pork rests, make the sauce. Place the orange juice, mango juice, agave syrup, vanilla bean and seeds, butter, and salt in a large saucepan and bring to a boil over high heat. Reduce the heat to medium-low and simmer until the sauce is syrupy, about 15 minutes. Remove and discard the vanilla bean.

7. Slice the rested loin into $1/2$- to $3/4$-inch-thick pieces. Arrange the pork on a serving platter, drizzle with the vanilla mango sauce, and serve.

SHORT RIBS *with* BAY-CURRANT SAUCE

Serves 6

- ½ cup currants
- ¾ cup dry white wine (such as pinot grigio)
- 1 yellow onion, roughly chopped
- 1 large red bell pepper, halved, seeded, and roughly chopped
- 1 jalapeño pepper, halved, seeded, and roughly chopped
- ¼ cup roughly chopped fresh cilantro
- 4 garlic cloves, roughly chopped
- 2 fresh ají dulce or jarred pickled cherry peppers
- ¼ cup extra-virgin olive oil
- 2 tablespoons Worcestershire sauce
- 1 teaspoon ground cumin
- 1 teaspoon dried oregano
- ½ teaspoon crushed bay leaves
- 1 tablespoon plus 1 teaspoon kosher salt
- ½ teaspoon freshly ground black pepper
- 4 pounds flanken-style crosscut bone-in short ribs
- ¼ cup vegetable oil
- ¼ cup sugar
- 4 cups Beef Stock (page 210) or store-bought beef broth

Asado negro, a beef roast cooked low and slow and turned black by caramelized sugar in wine and in panela (an unrefined block of sugar made from evaporated sugar cane juice), is one of the staple dishes of Venezuela. With this version, short ribs are marinated overnight in a puree of currants, wine, and aromatics like onions, garlic, and ají dulce and then cooked on the stove top until they are dark and fall-off-the-bone perfect. The dish is great with risotto or Vanilla Mashed Potatoes (see box, page 87).

1. Soak the currants in the white wine in a small bowl until they're plump and soft, 15 to 20 minutes. Transfer the currants and any remaining wine to the bowl of a food processor. Add the onions, bell peppers, jalapeño, cilantro, garlic, ají dulce, olive oil, Worcestershire sauce, cumin, oregano, bay leaves, 1 teaspoon of the salt, and the black pepper and process until completely smooth. Place the short ribs in a gallon-size resealable plastic bag, pour in the marinade, and turn the meat in the sauce to make sure it's evenly coated. Seal the bag and refrigerate overnight.

2. Heat the vegetable oil, sugar, and the remaining 1 tablespoon salt in a large pot over medium-high heat until the sugar begins to brown and caramelize, 4 to 5 minutes. Remove the ribs from the marinade, allowing the excess liquid to drip off (save the marinade for later), and place them meat side down in the pot. Cook the short ribs until they are browned, using tongs to constantly turn them so they don't burn, for about 10 minutes. Pour in the beef stock and the reserved marinade and bring the liquid to a boil over high heat, cooking until the liquid is slightly reduced, about 5 minutes.

continued

3. Reduce the heat to medium-low and simmer the short ribs until they're tender and a little crispy around the edges, about 1 hour, stirring every 20 minutes. Transfer the ribs to a serving dish and set aside. Increase the heat to medium-high and simmer the sauce until it is thick, about 10 minutes longer. Pour the sauce over the ribs, sprinkle with cilantro, and serve.

Sabes Qué?

Save time by making the short ribs in a pressure cooker. Follow the recipe as instructed, using an uncovered pressure cooker to brown the short ribs. After reducing the liquid slightly, place the cover on the pressure cooker and increase the heat to high. Once the pressure is brought up and stabilized (following the manufacturers' instructions), cook the short ribs until they're tender, 35 to 40 minutes. Follow the manufacturer's instructions to release the pressure and remove the lid to check the short ribs—if the meat is easily pulled from the bone, the ribs are done. Continue with the recipe as instructed.

vanilla mashed potatoes Reinvent standard mashed potatoes with the exotic flavor of vanilla bean. Follow your favorite recipe for mashed potatoes, cooking the potatoes as the recipe instructs. Bring the cream, half-and-half, or milk that you're using to make the mashed potatoes to a boil. Turn off the heat and add the butter. Split a vanilla bean in half lengthwise and use the back of a paring knife to scrape out the seeds. Add both the seeds and vanilla bean to the pot with the cream and butter, stir to combine, cover, and set aside to steep for 10 minutes. Remove and discard the split vanilla bean and pour the vanilla mixture over the cooked potatoes, mashing them to your taste. Stir in some salt and serve.

MAKE-AHEAD WILD MUSHROOM
and STEAK RISOTTO

- 2 tablespoons extra-virgin olive oil
- 1½ cups Arborio rice
- 3 cups hot Chicken Stock (page 211) or store-bought chicken broth
- 1½ ounces dried wild mushrooms (such as morels, porcinis, and shiitakes)
- 2½ cups red wine (such as merlot or cabernet sauvignon)
- 1 tablespoon truffle oil (optional)
- 1 shallot, very finely chopped
- 6 garlic cloves, very finely chopped
- ½ pound beef tenderloin (about 1 thick filet mignon), cut into ½-inch cubes
- 2 cups finely grated Parmigiano-Reggiano cheese
- 4 tablespoons (½ stick) unsalted butter
- 2 tablespoons finely chopped fresh flat-leaf parsley
- Thinly shaved fresh black truffle for serving (optional)

Risotto is very popular in Venezuela thanks to the large number of Italian immigrants in the country. It also happens to be one of the first dishes I learned how to cook. Later, on my restaurant's menu, there was always at least one kind of risotto made with whatever I happened to have on hand, from vegetables to seafood to just saffron. The trick to making risotto in a restaurant setting is to precook the rice component ahead of time—this is also the way to get risotto on the table if you're hosting a party and would prefer to mingle with your guests rather than stand over the stove for twenty minutes stirring rice. My grandmother on my father's side used to make the most wonderful risotto with dried mushrooms. My recipe plays off hers, but adds a few big-flavor ingredients like filet mignon and truffle oil to really send it over the top.

1. Heat 1 tablespoon of the olive oil in a large heavy-bottomed pot over medium-high heat. Add the rice and stir constantly while cooking until the rice has absorbed some of the oil, about 30 seconds. Pour in 2 cups of the hot chicken stock and cook the rice, stirring constantly, until the rice is partially cooked and has absorbed most of the broth, 12 to 15 minutes. Transfer the rice to a rimmed baking sheet and set aside to cool (if you are planning on cooking the risotto more than a few hours after cooking the rice, then cover the baking sheet with plastic wrap and refrigerate for up to 2 days).

2. Place the mushrooms in a medium bowl and cover with 2 cups of the red wine. Set aside until the mushrooms are soft and pliant, about 10 minutes. Drain the mushrooms through

continued

a fine-mesh sieve (discard the wine), roughly chop, and set aside.

3. Heat the remaining 1 tablespoon olive oil and the truffle oil, if using, in a large heavy-bottomed pot over medium-high heat. Add the shallots, garlic, and beef tenderloin and cook, stirring often, until the beef is browned, 2 to 3 minutes. Stir in the chopped mushrooms and cook until they're heated through, about 1 minute. Add the remaining $1/2$ cup red wine, cooking until the wine is reduced by half, about 3 minutes.

4. Stir in the precooked rice and add the remaining 1 cup chicken stock, $1/4$ cup at a time, stirring between additions, until the rice is al dente and the risotto is loose and creamy, 8 to 10 minutes longer. Stir in the Parmigiano-Reggiano cheese and the butter. Once they have melted, sprinkle with the parsley and truffles, if using, and serve.

BLUE CHEESE-CRUSTED BEEF TENDERLOIN
with PASSION FRUIT DEMI-GLAZE

Serves 4

FOR THE BEEF FILLETS

- 1 cup crumbled blue cheese
- 2 tablespoons unsalted butter
- 1 tablespoon Dijon mustard
- Four 6- to 8-ounce, 1¹/₂- to 2-inch-thick beef tenderloin fillets
- ¹/₂ teaspoon kosher salt
- ¹/₂ teaspoon freshly ground black pepper
- 2 tablespoon extra-virgin olive oil

FOR THE PASSION FRUIT DEMI-GLAZE

- 1 tablespoon extra-virgin olive oil
- ¹/₂ pound porcini or cremini mushrooms, stemmed and thinly sliced
- 1¹/₂ shallots, very finely chopped
- 6 garlic cloves, very finely minced
- 1 cup Simplified Red Wine Demi-Glaze (page 208)
- ¹/₂ cup passion fruit juice
- ¹/₄ cup agave syrup
- 2 tablespoons soy sauce

This dish was hands down the most popular dinner item I ever had on a menu at my restaurants and is perfect for any special occasion. It has a totally unique flavor with a Latin edge. Serve it with a side dish of spinach or mashed potatoes (see pages 87 and 79).

1. Before cooking the fillets, make a blue cheese butter. Place the blue cheese, butter, and Dijon mustard in the bowl of a food processor and blend until smooth. Scrape the mixture into a small bowl, cover the bowl with plastic wrap, and refrigerate for at least 20 minutes or up to overnight.

2. Set the fillets on a large plate. Season with the salt and pepper and then coat the fillets with the olive oil. Heat a large skillet over high heat for 2 minutes. Add the fillets and cook until a nice crust forms, 3 to 4 minutes on each side. Transfer the fillets to a clean plate (set the pan aside for the sauce) and set aside.

3. To make the glaze, pour the olive oil into the pan used to sear the fillets and place the pan over medium-high heat. Add the mushrooms, shallots, and garlic and cook, stirring often, until the mushrooms start to get glossy, about 3 minutes. Stir in the red wine demi-glaze, passion fruit juice, agave syrup, and soy sauce and bring to a boil. Reduce the heat to medium-low and let the glaze reduce until it's thick and syrupy, 35 to 40 minutes.

4. Preheat the oven to 400°F.

continued

5. Remove the blue cheese butter from the refrigerator. Line a rimmed baking sheet with aluminum foil and place the fillets on it. Top each fillet with 1 tablespoon of the blue cheese butter. Roast the fillets until the blue cheese is melted and the edges of the cheese begin to brown, about 10 minutes. Remove the fillets from the oven and place each one on a plate. Pour some passion fruit glaze around each fillet and serve.

Sabes Qué?

Incredibly tender and decadent beef tenderloin is fantastic, but for a more cost-friendly cut, try steaks like sirloin culotte, hanger steak, or top-loin club steak.

SUN-DRIED TOMATO BRÛLÉE

Serves 6

1¹⁄₃ cups (5 ounces) dry-packed sun-dried tomatoes

4¹⁄₂ ounces fresh goat cheese, crumbled (about ¹⁄₂ cup)

12 pitted black olives, roughly chopped

12 pitted green olives, roughly chopped

6 large egg yolks

3⁄4 cup plus 2 tablespoons milk

3⁄4 cup plus 2 tablespoons heavy cream

1 cup finely grated Parmigiano-Reggiano cheese

A savory custard of sweet and plump sun-dried tomatoes, pungent goat cheese, and green and black olives is finished with a layer of gorgeously browned Parmigiano-Reggiano cheese that gets brûléed under the broiler just before serving. You can serve this side dish next to the simplest protein—a pan-seared chicken breast or a piece of grilled fish—and it is instantly elevated to something more elegant. The custards can be baked ahead, cooled, and refrigerated for up to two days. Sprinkle them with the Parmigiano-Reggiano cheese and brown under the broiler just before serving.

1. Place the sun-dried tomatoes in a medium bowl and cover them with boiling water. Set aside for 10 minutes to rehydrate. Drain through a fine-mesh sieve and thinly slice the tomatoes crosswise into strips (discard the liquid).

2. Preheat the oven to 325°F. Set six 6-ounce ramekins in a 9 by 13-inch baking dish.

3. Divide the goat cheese evenly among the ramekins. Top with the black olives, green olives, and all but 12 slices of the sun-dried tomatoes. Set aside.

4. Bring a kettle of hot water to a boil, turn off the heat, and set aside. Whisk together the egg yolks in a medium heatproof bowl. Pour the milk into a small saucepan and bring to a boil over high heat. Whisk in the cream, and then slowly whisk about ¹⁄₄ cup of the hot milk mixture into the yolks. Continue to whisk in the hot milk mixture until it's completely incorporated. Pour the custard over the sun-dried tomato mixture in each ramekin.

5. Place the baking dish in the oven. Pour the hot water from the kettle into the baking dish until the water rises halfway up the sides of the ramekins. Bake the custards until the tops are barely firm to the touch (they should have a little bounce to them) and the custards jiggle when the ramekins are tapped, about 35 minutes.

6. Carefully remove the baking dish from the oven. Using tongs, transfer the ramekins to a wire rack to cool completely, about 20 minutes.

7. Adjust an oven rack to the upper-middle position and heat the broiler to high.

8. Transfer the custards from the wire rack to a rimmed baking sheet. Sprinkle about $2^1/_2$ tablespoons of the Parmigiano-Reggiano cheese over the surface of each custard. Place the baking sheet in the oven and broil the tops until they're golden brown, about 5 minutes (check the custards often as broiler intensities vary). Remove the baking sheet from the oven and use tongs to transfer the ramekins to small plates. Place 2 strips of sun-dried tomatoes over the top of each custard and serve.

AFUERA!
MOVE YOUR KITCHEN TABLE OUTSIDE

This chapter is all about preparing and enjoying food outdoors. It combines the ease of no-cook recipes like guacamole and Cucumber Carpaccio with Dijon Vinaigrette, where you simply assemble a dish rather than cook it, with no-fuss grilling favorites. And you can't get more South American than grilling or cooking *a la parrilla* as we say. The most important ingredient in Latin-style grilled food is the taste of the smoky char from the grill, which is why grilled food is kept simple. Salt and pepper are often the seasonings of choice; that said, I have developed a true love of sticky-sweet barbecue sauce, especially when slathered on smoky, succulent baby back ribs!

Truth be told, vegetables have never been a focus of the Latin grill, but I've devised some unique ways to serve grilled vegetables that make them just as delectable as their meaty counterparts.

Grilling is always about sitting down with my best friends and family to eat a delicious and flavorful meal *al fresco*, surrounded by the beautiful smell of char-grilled goodness. It just doesn't get any better than that.

SEARED TUNA TAQUITOS IN BIBB WRAPS
with TOMATO-AVOCADO SALSITA

Serves 4

Four 6-ounce, 1-inch-thick tuna fillets, skin removed
1 tablespoon extra-virgin olive oil
1 teaspoon kosher salt
1/2 teaspoon freshly ground black pepper
8 large Bibb lettuce leaves
1/2 cup Tomato-Avocado Salsita (page 101)
4 sprigs fresh cilantro (tender stems only)
1 lime, cut into wedges

In these taquitos, I replace the customary tortilla with a Southeast Asian–style lettuce wrap that satisfies taco cravings in a totally light, refreshing, and flavorful way. The crispness of the lettuce pairs nicely with the creaminess of the avocado. Try making a platter of fast and tasty Bibb-wrapped taquitos with the other fish taquito fillings on pages 101 and 104.

1. Place the tuna fillets in a large bowl. Drizzle with the olive oil and rub it into both sides. Season with the salt and pepper, and set aside.

2. Prepare a hot charcoal or gas grill.

3. Place the tuna on the grill and cook each side just until there are grill marks, about 1 minute per side (you want the center of the tuna to remain rare). Carefully transfer the tuna to a clean cutting board and slice crosswise into 1/2-inch-thick pieces.

4. Place the lettuce leaves on a serving platter and top each with some tuna. Drizzle some tomato-avocado salsita over the tuna, and serve with cilantro and a lime wedge.

Sabes Qué?

Get your lettuce wraps extra crisp by washing them and placing the still-wet leaves on a paper towel–lined plate. Refrigerate the leaves for up to 20 minutes to get them nice and cold and crunchy.

SMASHED GUACAMOLE

Serves 8

½ cup finely chopped fresh cilantro

1 jalapeño pepper, halved, seeded, deveined, and finely chopped (optional)

1 garlic clove, finely minced

Juice of 1 lime

1 tablespoon kosher salt, plus more to taste

4 Hass avocados, halved, pitted, peeled, and finely diced

1 small red onion, finely chopped

¼ teaspoon freshly ground black pepper, plus more to taste

1 small tomato, finely chopped

You will never guess where I got the inspiration for my guacamole—Thailand! It's funny, especially with my coming from South America, that I had to fly halfway around the world to find the secret to great guacamole. The key is in the technique. When I was in Bangkok, I learned how to make this incredible spicy-sour sauce for sticky rice, and the trick was to make a paste from the chiles, garlic, cilantro, and salt before adding fish sauce and lemon juice. By mashing the aromatic ingredients first I released the essential oils, and it was like an explosion of freshness and exciting tastes. It takes just a minute to mash up the base, but the results are incredible. The herby creaminess of the guacamole works nicely with anything crunchy or bready, like telitas (see page 131), tortilla chips, or Venezuelan Arepas (page 30)—or for a healthy crunch, cucumber, celery, and carrot sticks. It keeps for a few hours in the refrigerator—just stir before serving.

Place one-quarter of the cilantro, one-half of the jalapeño, the garlic, lime juice, and salt in a mortar with a pestle (you can also use a small bowl and a fork to make the paste). Smash all of the ingredients together until the mixture looks juicy and like a rough paste. Add the avocados, onions, the remaining jalapeño, and the black pepper to the bowl. Stir and smash to the consistency and texture you like best (I like mine chunky). Stir in the remaining cilantro and the tomatoes, taste, and season with salt and pepper as needed. Use a rubber spatula to scrape the guacamole into a serving bowl and serve.

GRILLED SALMON TAQUITOS *with* TOMATO-AVOCADO SALSITA

FOR THE TOMATO-AVOCADO SALSITA

- 1 small tomato
- 1/2 small red onion, very finely chopped
- 1/2 cup finely chopped fresh cilantro
- 2 Hass avocados, halved, pitted, peeled, and finely chopped
- Juice of 1 lime
- 1 teaspoon kosher salt

FOR THE SALMON

- Three 8-ounce salmon fillets, skin removed
- 1 tablespoon extra-virgin olive oil
- 1 teaspoon kosher salt
- 1 teaspoon freshly ground black pepper
- 8 Cheesy Telitas Flatbread (page 131), or eight 6-inch store-bought corn tortillas, or homemade Herb Tortillas (page 203)
- 1 cup baby greens (such as arugula or spinach)
- 1 lime, cut into 8 wedges

When you start with a beautiful piece of salmon, it doesn't take much to bring out its best flavors—just season with salt and pepper and quickly grill so it stays medium-rare in the middle. To turn it into a taquito, wrap it in a flatbread, soft tortilla, or a telita and finish it off with a squeeze of fresh lime juice and a dollop of this citrusy, creamy tomato-avocado salsita. These taquitos are also excellent topped with a drizzle of the Roasted Habanero Salsita (page 197). When buying salmon, give it a good once-over—it should glisten and look firm without any hint of softness.

1. To make the salsita, bring a small saucepan of water to a boil over high heat. Use a paring knife to slice an X in the bottom of the tomato and then blanch the tomato in the boiling water until the skin at the bottom of the tomato starts to curl, 1 to 2 minutes. Use a slotted spoon to transfer the tomato to a small bowl of ice water. Once the tomato is cool enough to handle, peel off the skin and discard. Halve the tomato, seed it, and finely chop it. Place it in a small bowl, add the onions and cilantro, cover the bowl with plastic wrap, and set aside. Place the avocados in a medium bowl and gently toss with the lime juice and salt. Cover the bowl with plastic wrap and set aside.

2. To make the salmon, place the fillets in a large bowl. Drizzle with the olive oil and rub the oil into the fish. Season with the salt and pepper and set aside.

3. Prepare a hot charcoal or gas grill.

4. Place the salmon on the grill and cook until browned, about 1 minute. Use a spatula to carefully flip over the fillets

continued

and grill the other side until browned, about 1 minute longer. Carefully remove the salmon fillets from the grill and gently slice them crosswise into strips.

5. Warm the telitas or tortillas on the grill on both sides just until they're pliable and slightly charred. Transfer them to a serving platter. Place some baby greens on top of each one and top each with grilled salmon strips. Add the tomato-cilantro mixture to the avocados and gently stir to combine. Divide the salsita among the taquitos and serve with a lime wedge.

Light My Fire: How to Get Your Grill On

Getting a grill good and hot is key to successful grilling. If you are using a gas grill, turn all burners to high, cover the grill for 10 minutes, and then uncover it to scrape the grates with a wire brush. Clean the grates of any stuck-on debris and then adjust the heat as the recipe instructs.

If you are using a charcoal grill, light the coals using a chimney starter or lighter fluid. If using a chimney starter, fill the chimney three-quarters full with coals and place some bunched up sheets of newspaper underneath the chimney. Set the chimney on the lower grill rack (set the upper grill rack aside for the time being), light the paper, and let the outer edges of the coals turn white-gray before turning them out onto the bottom grate. If using lighter fluid, just douse the coals with the fluid and light. In either case, once the coals are white-hot, use long tongs to adjust them as necessary (banking them to one side to create a medium and hot side of the grill, for example). Place the upper grill grate on the grill, let it get nice and hot, and then use a wire grill brush to clean the grate.

If using gas and the grill becomes too hot or cold while you're cooking, simply adjust the level of the heat. To cool off a too-hot charcoal fire, you can spread out the coals into a thinner layer or push them to one side to relieve one side from the intense heat (creating a two-level fire, good for searing meat on the hot side and letting it cook through on the cooler side). You can also close the vents at the bottom of the grill to limit the oxygen supply to the fire, which will make the heat less intense. If you need to add heat to your charcoal fire, toss in a few extra coals.

SNAPPER TAQUITOS
with JICAMA-APPLE SALSITA

Serves 4

1 pound skinless red snapper fillets

1 tablespoon extra-virgin olive oil

1½ teaspoons kosher salt

1½ teaspoons freshly ground black pepper

8 Herb Tortillas (page 203) or eight 6-inch store-bought corn tortillas

2 cups thinly sliced radicchio (optional)

2 cups Jicama-Apple Salsita (page 195)

1 lime, cut into wedges

A day at the beach with friends in Puerto Vallarta or Los Roques, an archipelago of fifty islands off the coast of Venezuela, is the ultimate getaway treat. After a long hot day in the sun, we kick back with icy-cold *micheladas* (Bloody Marys made with beer instead of vodka) and lots and lots of grilled taquitos. We'll grill fresh fish like snapper or tuna and serve it up with an assortment of salsitas, mixing and matching them with the fish to suit our taste. The jicama-apple salsita is especially nice because it is so fresh and crunchy, a great counterpoint to the delicate texture and smoky flavor of grilled fish. Grouper, snapper, tilapia, sea bass, salmon, and tuna all grill beautifully, so feel free to buy the freshest fish you can find without worrying about straying from the recipe.

1. Place the snapper fillets in a medium bowl. Drizzle the olive oil over the fillets and rub it into both sides. Season with the salt and pepper and set aside.

2. Prepare a hot charcoal or gas grill.

3. Place the snapper fillets on the grill and cook until they are golden brown, about 3 minutes. Use a spatula to carefully flip them, grilling the other side until golden brown, another 3 minutes. Carefully remove the fillets from the grill and slice crosswise into strips.

4. Stack the tortillas and wrap them in a damp kitchen towel. Place them on a plate and microwave them in 20-second increments until they're fragrant and warmed, about 1 minute. Place the tortillas on a serving platter and top with some radicchio, if using, and then the grilled snapper strips. Cover each taquito with about ¼ cup jicama-apple salsita and serve with a lime wedge.

a taquito party   Small tacos are a crowd-pleaser, especially my party-friendly taquitos, which are just the right size for entertaining and cocktails. Getting three, four, or five
different taquitos on a plate delivers a range of flavors and textures. First, lay out several
kinds of tortillas on the table. Then, grill up a few different kinds of fish, set out some
salsitas, and you're done! It's a great way to entertain because everyone gets involved, it's
fun, and it's very little stress on the host. Mix and match a few items from each category
below, and don't forget lots of lime wedges for serving.

TORTILLAS (Corn, Flour, Whole Wheat)

Herb (page 203)
Corn
Flour (use a biscuit cutter
   to cut out smaller
   circles)
Cheesy Telitas Flatbread
   (page 203)

FISH

Grouper
Salmon (page 101)
Snapper (page 104)
Sea Bass
Tuna (page 99)
Tilapia

SALSITAS

Jicama-Apple Salsita
   (page 195)
Tomato-Avocado Salsita
   (see page 99)
Spicy Guasacaca Salsita
   (page 194)
Cilantro and Roasted
   Jalapeño Salsa Picante
   (page 196)
Roasted Habanero Salsita
   (page 197)

TROPICAL SESAME SHRIMP MARTINIS

Serves 6

FOR THE SESAME VINAIGRETTE

- 3 tablespoons rice vinegar
- 3 tablespoons soy sauce
- 2½ teaspoons fresh lemon juice
- 2½ teaspoons sugar
- ¾ teaspoon prepared dry mustard
  Pinch of kosher salt
- 3 large shallots, very finely chopped
- 3 tablespoons light sesame oil
- 3 tablespoons vegetable oil

FOR THE SHRIMP

- 2 oranges
- 2 pounds small cooked shrimp
- 1 cup hearts of palm, rinsed, drained, halved lengthwise, and sliced crosswise into ¼-inch-thick rounds
- 1 cup cherry tomatoes, quartered
- 3 cups baby greens (such as arugula or baby spinach)
- 6 small sprigs fresh cilantro

Simple and chic, this is a fast and easy starter or light meal. Thanks to fresh-cooked shrimp sold at most grocery stores, this dish can be assembled in minutes. The *palmitos* (hearts of palm) are a very Latin addition to this otherwise Asian-inspired recipe—they give a great al dente contrast to the plump, juicy-sweet mandarin segments and the cooked shrimp. If you prefer, you can boil raw shrimp in water flavored with lemon juice, just until pink (I'm partial to shrimp from the Florida Keys or the Gulf Coast) instead of using precooked shrimp.

1. To make the vinaigrette, whisk together the rice vinegar, soy sauce, lemon juice, 1½ tablespoons of water, the sugar, dry mustard, and salt in a medium bowl. Whisk in the shallots and then add the sesame oil and vegetable oil, whisking slowly to emulsify the vinaigrette.

2. To make the shrimp, place the oranges on a cutting board. Slice off the tops and bottoms to expose the fruit and then slice away the peel and white pith. Use a sharp paring knife to slice between the orange membranes, releasing the orange segments. Transfer the oranges to a large bowl and add the shrimp, hearts of palm, and cherry tomatoes. Pour the sesame vinaigrette over the mixture and gently toss with your hands to combine.

3. Divide the baby greens among six martini glasses (or small plates). Top with the shrimp salad and finish with a cilantro sprig. Serve immediately.

CHICKEN *and* ALMOND PESTO SLIDERS

Serves 4

FOR THE ALMOND PESTO

- 3/4 cup extra-virgin olive oil
- 1 generous cup sliced almonds, roughly chopped
- 1 cup grated Parmigiano-Reggiano cheese
- 2 tablespoons finely chopped fresh basil
- 2 garlic cloves, very finely minced

FOR THE CHICKEN SLIDERS

- 2 tablespoons vegetable oil
- 1 large egg
- 1 pound boneless, skinless chicken breasts, cut into 1/2-inch cubes
- 1/2 jalapeño pepper, halved, seeded, deveined, and finely chopped
- 2 scallions, white and light green parts only, finely chopped
- 1 tablespoon finely chopped fresh cilantro
- 1 teaspoon kosher salt
- 3 tablespoons dried unseasoned bread crumbs
- 6 ounces mozzarella, sliced into 4 rounds
- 4 small brioche buns or mini buns
- 1 tomato, sliced into 1/4-inch-thick rounds

These mini-burgers feature jalapeños, scallions, and cilantro and are topped with melted mozzarella and a rich basil-almond pesto. The almond pesto gives the burger great texture and freshness. Formed uncooked burgers can be frozen in a resealable freezer bag for up to three weeks. Thaw in the fridge overnight and then grill as instructed.

1. To make the almond pesto, whisk together the olive oil, almonds, Parmigiano-Reggiano cheese, basil, and garlic in a medium bowl and set aside.

2. To make the sliders, pour the vegetable oil into a large bowl and whisk in the egg. Add the chicken, the jalapeño, scallions, cilantro, and salt and stir to combine. Stir in the bread crumbs and then divide the mixture into 4 balls. Slightly flatten each ball into a 1 1/2-inch-thick patty and set aside.

3. Prepare a hot charcoal or gas grill.

4. Grill the burgers until they are golden brown on one side, about 5 minutes. Flip over the burgers and place a mozzarella round on top of the burger. Cook until the underside is golden brown and the cheese is melted, about 5 minutes longer.

5. While the burgers cook, toast the buns. Place the buns cut side down on the grill (or an upper grill rack if your grill has one) until toasted, about 2 minutes. Remove the buns and burgers from the grill.

6. Place a burger on each bun bottom. Top with a tomato slice and then spoon some almond pesto on top. Cover with the top half of the bun and serve.

VARIATION: *Pistachio Pesto Slider Lettuce Wraps*

Substitute shelled pistachios for the almonds in the pesto. Overlap two Bibb lettuce leaves on a plate and place the burger on top. Add the tomato slices and some pesto and serve.

CUCUMBER CARPACCIO
with DIJON VINAIGRETTE

1 large unpeeled cucumber, trimmed

Juice of 1 lemon

1½ teaspoons Dijon mustard

1 garlic clove, very finely minced

¼ teaspoon freshly ground pink peppercorns

¼ cup extra-virgin olive oil

1 leek, trimmed, white part only, finely chopped

One 2- to 3-ounce block Parmigiano-Reggiano cheese, shaved with a mandoline or vegetable peeler

¼ cup chervil leaves

I am always looking for unexpected ways to serve fresh vegetables that are tangy, crunchy, refreshing, and exciting to eat. This supersimple twist on beef carpaccio utilizes an inexpensive mandoline to slice the cucumbers into thin rounds which you then dress with a quick peppercorn vinaigrette. You don't even need to turn on the oven or heat a pan to make this hot weather pleaser.

1. Using a mandoline or a sharp knife, slice the cucumber into very thin rounds. Divide the rounds among four plates, layering them in a circle.

2. Whisk together the lemon juice, mustard, garlic, ground peppercorns, and 2 tablespoons of water in a small bowl. Slowly whisk in the olive oil until the vinaigrette is thick and emulsified. Drizzle the vinaigrette over each plate of cucumbers. Garnish with the leeks, shaved Parmigiano-Reggiano cheese, and chervil and serve immediately.

DESIGNER MANGO-JERK CHICKEN SALAD

Serves 6

2 tablespoons Caribbean jerk seasoning

2 tablespoons extra-virgin olive oil

8 chicken cutlets

1½ cups mango chunks (½ to ¾ inch)

1 cup light mayonnaise

2 cups Caramelized Walnuts (page 212)

4 cups baby greens

This recipe was so popular at my first restaurant, Food Café, that people started calling it the "designer" salad, after Miami's Design District (where the restaurant was located), and actually wrote me letters begging for the recipe. The combination of spicy chicken, fresh greens, crunchy caramelized walnuts, and sweet mangoes is like the personality of Miami on a plate. Try it served in a pineapple (see page 114) or turned into a deliciously hearty sandwich. The chicken needs to marinate in the spices overnight, so plan accordingly.

1. Whisk together the jerk seasoning and olive oil in a medium bowl (or shake together in a gallon-size resealable plastic bag). Add the chicken and turn to coat in the seasoned oil. Cover the bowl with plastic wrap and refrigerate overnight.

2. Prepare a hot charcoal or gas grill.

3. Grill the chicken until both sides are marked and the chicken is cooked through, about 3 minutes per side. Transfer the chicken to a cutting board and set aside until the chicken is completely cooled, about 10 minutes, before slicing crosswise into thin strips.

4. Stir together the mangoes and mayonnaise in a large bowl. Add the walnuts and chicken strips and gently stir to coat. Cover the bowl with plastic wrap and refrigerate until chilled.

5. Divide the baby greens among six plates. Top each plate with some of the chicken salad and serve.

continued

VARIATION: *Designer Mango–Jerk Chicken Salad in a Pineapple*

Make the chicken salad as instructed. Stir $1\frac{1}{2}$ cups finely chopped fresh pineapple chunks into the salad along with $\frac{1}{3}$ cup shredded unsweetened coconut. Serve in a pineapple boat (see below) with a few strawberry slices on top.

making a pineapple boat

Making a pineapple boat takes a few minutes, but it's a great presentation trick to know. You can fill it with chicken salad, a fruit salad, or even a simple green salad.

Place a fresh ripe pineapple on a cutting board and slice the top quarter off lengthwise, exposing the golden fruit and leaving the spiky top intact. Wrap the thin piece of pineapple in plastic wrap and save for another use. Carve out the interior of the pineapple, leaving a $\frac{1}{2}$-inch perimeter around the edges of the skin. Cut deeply, but don't let the knife cut through the skin on the bottom of the pineapple. Slice through the interior lengthwise at 1-inch intervals and then crosswise at 1-inch intervals. Using a grapefruit spoon, scoop out the pineapple chunks, leaving the hollowed pineapple shell behind. (Trim the chunks into smaller cubes if making the tropical chicken salad above). Fill the pineapple boat with chicken salad or fruit salad.

CITRUS *and* CERVEZA CHICKEN

Serves 4

FOR THE HERB BUTTER

- 2 tablespoons unsalted butter, at room temperature
- 2 tablespoons extra-virgin olive oil
- 1/2 cup finely chopped fresh flat-leaf parsley
- 1/4 cup finely chopped fresh basil
- 1/4 cup finely chopped fresh cilantro
- 2 tablespoons finely chopped fresh thyme

FOR THE CHICKEN

- 1 medium yellow onion, quartered and sliced crosswise
- 1 carrot, halved and sliced crosswise
- 1/2 celery stalk, thinly sliced
- 5 fresh thyme sprigs
- 1 garlic clove, thinly sliced
- 1 lemon, halved crosswise, one-half sliced into 1/2-inch-thick rounds
- 1/2 orange, sliced crosswise into 1/2-inch-thick rounds
- One 3 1/2- to 4-pound chicken
- 1 teaspoon kosher salt
- 1/2 teaspoon freshly ground black pepper
- One 24-ounce can beer (any kind will do)
- 1/2 cup fresh orange juice

This recipe for beer-can chicken not only makes an incredibly herby chicken, but it's supermoist and juicy with beautiful crisp skin, too. The beer essentially steams the chicken with moisture from the inside. The acid in the lemon juice makes the skin crisp and gorgeous while the herb butter, packed with parsley, basil, cilantro, and thyme, is all about big, bold, fresh flavor. Serve with Tomato-Avocado Salsita (page 99).

1. Prepare a medium-hot charcoal or gas grill. Close the lid and bring the temperature to 400°F.

2. To make the herb butter, place the butter, olive oil, parsley, basil, cilantro, and thyme in the bowl of a food processor and blend until smooth. Set aside.

3. To make the chicken, place the onions, carrots, celery, thyme, garlic, lemons, and oranges in the bottom of an 8-inch square disposable aluminum pan and toss with your hands to combine. Clear a circle in the middle of the pan (this is where you'll set the chicken) and set the pan aside.

4. Rinse the chicken under cold running water and then squeeze the remaining lemon half over the chicken. Pat the chicken dry with paper towels. Rub the chicken with the salt and pepper and then use a rubber spatula (or your hands) to rub the surface of the chicken with the herb butter.

5. Place the aluminum pan with the vegetables on the grill. Pop open the top of the beer can and stand the chicken on top of it so the beer can is in the cavity of the chicken. Place the chicken upright in the middle of the aluminum pan. Use your hands to gather the vegetables around the beer can. Pour the orange juice over the vegetables, close the lid to the grill, and

continued

roast the chicken until the juices in the leg/thigh joint run clear and the temperature of the chicken in the meatiest part of the thigh reads 165°F, about 1¹/₂ hours.

6. Using tongs and kitchen towels, carefully remove the chicken and beer can from the roasting pan and place the chicken and can on a cutting board. Hold the beer can with tongs or a thick wad of paper towels and then carefully twist off the chicken, placing it back on the cutting board (discard the beer can). Tent the chicken with aluminum foil and set aside for 10 minutes. Discard the vegetables in the roasting pan. Carve the chicken and serve.

MANGO BBQ BABY BACK RIBS

Serves 8

FOR THE RIBS

- 4 racks baby back pork ribs
- 2 teaspoons Caribbean jerk seasoning
- 2 teaspoons ground coriander
- 2 teaspoons dried thyme
- 2 teaspoons sweet paprika
- 1 teaspoon kosher salt

FOR THE BARBECUE SAUCE

- 2 tablespoons unsalted butter
- 2 celery stalks, finely chopped
- 2 leeks, white and light green parts only, finely chopped
- 1 large yellow onion, finely chopped
- 2 garlic cloves, very finely chopped
- 2¹/₂ cups mango juice
- 2 cups ketchup
- 1¹/₂ cups Beef Stock (page 210) or store-bought beef broth
- ¹/₂ cup passion fruit juice
- ¹/₂ cup champagne vinegar
- ¹/₄ cup distilled white vinegar
- ¹/₄ cup fresh lemon juice (from about 1¹/₂ lemons)
- ¹/₄ cup Simplified Red Wine Demi-Glaze (page 208)
- ¹/₄ cup dark rum
- 2 tablespoons spicy Asian chili sauce
- 3 tablespoons Worcestershire sauce
- 1 teaspoon prepared dry mustard
- 1 teaspoon ground cinnamon
- 1 teaspoon kosher salt

These ribs are killer! The spices in the dry rub, including jerk seasoning, coriander, and thyme, infuse the meat, while dedicated basting with the homemade mango barbecue sauce (also fantastic with grilled chicken and pork chops) makes them finger-licking sticky-sweet amazing. I was inspired to create the combination dry rub marinade by my friend and cohost of *America's Next Great Restaurant*, Curtis Stone. It's a great idea, and I love how it builds flavor into the ribs twice (the ribs are infused with the dry rub for two hours or up to overnight, and then get a second marinade in the barbecue sauce for two hours before they even hit the grill). Cooking the ribs low and slow ensures that they'll be fall-off-the-bone tender. These can be baked up to one day ahead of time, refrigerated, and then finished on the grill.

1. Rinse the racks of ribs under cold running water and then pat them dry. Stir together the jerk seasoning, coriander, thyme, paprika, and salt in a small bowl. Add the ribs and rub the spices all over both sides of each rack. Place a sheet of aluminum foil on the counter, place a rack of ribs on top, and enclose with the foil (wrap the rack so the opening seam of the foil is on top of the rack). Repeat with the other 3 racks and refrigerate them for at least 2 hours or overnight.

2. To make the barbecue sauce, melt the butter in a medium pot over medium heat. Add the celery, leeks, onions, and garlic and cook until the onions start to soften, 4 to 5 minutes. Stir in the mango juice, ketchup, beef stock, passion fruit juice, champagne vinegar, white vinegar, lemon juice, red wine demi-glaze, rum, chili sauce, Worcestershire sauce, mus-

continued

tard, cinnamon, and salt. Increase the heat to high and bring to a boil. Reduce the heat to medium-low and simmer until the sauce is syrupy and reduced by half, about 2 hours.

3. Preheat the oven to 350°F.

4. Remove the racks from the refrigerator, place them on two rimmed baking sheets, and cook for 1 hour. Remove the pans from the oven, open the foil packets, and drain off any accumulated juices. Pour 1 cup of the barbecue sauce into a small bowl and use a pastry brush to brush both sides of each rack with some of the sauce. Reseal the foil packets and refrigerate the ribs for 2 hours.

5. Prepare a medium-hot charcoal or gas grill.

6. While the grill heats up, remove the ribs from the refrigerator, place on a work surface, and open the foil packets. Pour another 1 cup of barbecue sauce into a small bowl and use it to baste both sides of each rack. Let the ribs sit out at room temperature for at least 15 minutes.

7. Pour 2¹/₂ cups of the barbecue sauce into a medium bowl. When the grill is hot, place each rack on the grill bone side down and baste the top with barbecue sauce. Grill until the edges of the ribs are crisp and charred, about 15 minutes, basting the tops of the racks with about ¹/₂ cup of barbecue sauce every 3 minutes.

8. Heat the remaining barbecue sauce (about 1¹/₂ cups) in a small saucepan over medium-high heat. Remove the racks from the grill and slice them into 8 half racks. Serve with the warm barbecue sauce on the side.

GARLICKY GRILL-ROASTED BEETS
and POTATOES

2 golden beets, peeled and cut into 1-inch cubes

2 red beets, peeled and cut into 1-inch cubes

2 large potatoes (preferably Peruvian purple potatoes; Yukon gold or red potatoes work, too), peeled and cut into 1-inch cubes

1/3 cup extra-virgin olive oil

6 garlic cloves, very finely minced

3/4 cup finely chopped fresh cilantro

1 tablespoon finely chopped fresh thyme

1 1/2 tablespoons kosher salt

1 tablespoon freshly ground black pepper

Like tomatoes and corn, potatoes are indigenous to South America. Grill-roasted with red and golden beets, garlic, and olive oil, the potatoes here take on a sweet earthiness with a hint of smoke. Finished with bright green cilantro, this side dish is almost as good to look at as it is to eat it!

1. If using a gas grill, heat to medium-high, leaving the center burner turned off. If using a charcoal grill, bank the coals to one side and build a hot fire.

2. Place the golden beets, red beets, potatoes, olive oil, garlic, 1/4 cup of the cilantro, the thyme, salt, and pepper in a 9 by 13-inch disposable aluminum pan and toss the vegetables to evenly coat.

3. Place the aluminum pan on the grill (if using a charcoal grill, place it over the side without coals) and cover. Maintain a 400°F temperature until the beets and potatoes can be easily pierced with a paring knife, about 30 minutes. Remove the pan from the grill. Transfer the vegetables to a serving platter, sprinkle with the remaining 1/2 cup cilantro, and serve.

Sabes Qué?

This dish works beautifully in an indoor oven, too. Roast the vegetables at 400°F until a paring knife easily slips into the beets and potatoes, about 35 minutes, stirring halfway through roasting.

CHURRASCO STEAK *and* ARUGULA *with* CANDIED PEPPER CHIMICHURRI

Serves 4

FOR THE CHIMICHURRI

- 1/2 cup finely minced Candied Red Peppers (about 1/2 recipe, page 201)
- 1/4 cup candied pepper liquid
- 1/4 cup brine-packed capers, rinsed and finely chopped
- 1/4 cup finely chopped fresh flat-leaf parsley
- 2 tablespoons finely chopped fresh cilantro
- 6 garlic cloves, very finely minced
- 2 shallots, very finely chopped
- 1/2 cup extra-virgin olive oil

FOR THE STEAKS

- **Four 8-ounce skirt steaks**
- 2 tablespoons plus 1/2 teaspoon coarse sea salt
- 1 tablespoon plus 1/8 teaspoon freshly ground black pepper
- 3 tablespoons extra-virgin olive oil
- 1 tablespoon fresh lemon juice

- 4 cups baby arugula
- 1 cup halved cherry tomatoes

In Latin America, *churrasco* is a term used to define a thin, boneless cut of meat that cooks quickly on the grill. Most often we're talking skirt steak—it is marbled with fat, giving it a huge, meaty flavor and lots of juiciness. Churrasco steak is usually served with chimichurri, a classic vinegary parsley-garlic-oregano sauce. I give it a twist by adding candied peppers for a tangy-sweet-sour kick.

1. To make the chimichurri, place the candied peppers in a medium bowl with their liquid, capers, parsley, cilantro, garlic, and shallots and whisk to combine. Slowly whisk in the olive oil until the mixture is thick and emulsified. Set aside.

2. Prepare a hot charcoal or gas grill.

3. Season both sides of the skirt steaks with 2 tablespoons of the salt and 1 tablespoon of the black pepper and set on the grill. Cook without moving until there are grill marks, about 5 minutes. Turn over the steaks and cook the other side until there are grill marks and the steaks are cooked to your liking, about 3 minutes for medium-rare, 4 minutes for medium, and 5 minutes longer for medium-well. Use tongs to transfer the steaks to a large platter and set aside.

4. While the steaks rest, whisk together the olive oil, lemon juice, the remaining 1/2 teaspoon salt, and the remaining 1/8 teaspoon black pepper in a large bowl. Add the arugula and cherry tomatoes and gently toss to coat.

5. Arrange the 4 steaks on a large platter in a circular shape. Fill the center of the circle with the arugula and tomatoes and serve with the chimichurri on the side.

BALSAMIC GRILLED VEGETABLES

Serves 6

1 large head garlic, top third sliced off to expose the garlic cloves

1/4 cup plus 1 teaspoon extra-virgin olive oil

1 bunch medium-thick asparagus, tough ends snapped off

1 large zucchini, trimmed and cut on the diagonal into slices 3 to 4 inches long and 1/4 inch thick

1 large yellow summer squash, trimmed and cut on the diagonal into slices 3 to 4 inches long and 1/4 inch thick

1 large red bell pepper, halved, seeded, and sliced lengthwise into 2-inch-wide strips

1 large yellow bell pepper, halved, seeded, and sliced lengthwise into 2-inch-wide strips

1 large green bell pepper, halved, seeded, and sliced lengthwise into 2-inch-wide strips

2 tablespoons balsamic vinegar

1 1/2 teaspoons kosher salt, plus more to taste

3/4 teaspoon freshly ground black pepper, plus more to taste

1 fresh baguette, sliced

Letting vegetables hang out in a balsamic marinade for a little while before grilling them introduces a wonderful garlicky sweetness that even nonvegetable lovers cannot resist. Keep the vegetable strips long and thin and place them diagonally across the grill so they cook quickly and don't slip through the grates. The most important thing to keep in mind is to slice all of the vegetables evenly so they cook through at the same time. I usually make a double batch so I have leftovers for lunch the next day—the roasted vegetables are excellent served piled on a fresh baguette and drizzled with a little salsita over the top. The grill-roasted garlic is an extra bonus. Try it spread on crusty bread and eat along with the veggies, or with just about anything, for that matter.

1. Prepare a hot charcoal or gas grill.
2. Place the garlic in the center of a 6-inch square of aluminum foil so the exposed cloves face up. Drizzle 1 teaspoon of the olive oil over the exposed cloves and bring the corners of the foil up to the top of the head, gathering them together to seal the packet. Place the packet on the grill.
3. Place the asparagus in a medium bowl. Place the zucchini and yellow squash in another medium bowl. Place the sliced bell peppers in a third medium bowl.
4. In a small bowl, whisk together the remaining 1/4 cup olive oil, the vinegar, salt, and pepper. Drizzle one-third of the mixture over the asparagus, one-third over the zucchini and yellow squash, and one-third over the bell peppers, tossing to evenly coat the vegetables with the vinaigrette. Season with salt and black pepper.

111

5. Transfer the vegetables to the grill by lifting them out of the vinaigrette and letting any excess drip off. Place them on the grill so that all of the asparagus is on one-third of the grill, the zucchini and yellow squash on another third of the grill, and the bell peppers on the last third of the grill.

6. Cook the asparagus for about 5 minutes total, turning halfway through cooking, until the spears are somewhat limp and charred. Use tongs to transfer them from the grill to a serving platter. Cook the zucchini and yellow squash until both sides are grill marked and the squash is tender, about 4 minutes on each side. Cook the bell peppers until both sides are grill marked and the slices are somewhat limp, about 5 minutes on each side. Remove the garlic from the grill.

7. Place the bread slices on the grill to lightly toast for a minute or two. Serve the vegetables warm or at room temperature with the roasted garlic and grilled bread on the side.

SMOKY GRILLED BRUSSELS SPROUTS *with* PARMIGIANO-REGGIANO RIBBONS

Serves 4

10 ounces Brussels sprouts (about 3 cups), stems trimmed, halved

2 tablespoons Spicy Cherry Pepper Oil (page 198) or extra-virgin olive oil

1 tablespoon fresh lemon juice

1/2 shallot, sliced into 1/8-inch matchsticks

3 garlic cloves, sliced into 1/8-inch matchsticks

1 1/2 teaspoons kosher salt

2 ounces Parmigiano-Reggiano cheese, shaved with a vegetable peeler into ribbons (optional)

While many recipes call for boiling or roasting these mini heads of cabbage, grilling gives Brussels sprouts a smoky richness. Parmigiano-Reggiano cheese, garlic, and shallots also boost their earthy flavor.

1. Prepare a hot charcoal or gas grill. Place a large, shallow disposable aluminum pan on the grill top.

2. Place the Brussels sprouts, cherry pepper oil, lemon juice, shallots, garlic, and salt in a large bowl and toss to combine. Turn them out into the hot pan and cook until they're just al dente and beginning to wilt, 2 to 3 minutes. Use a wide spatula to flip the halved sprouts, letting the other side get color before transferring them to a serving bowl. Top with the Parmigiano-Reggiano ribbons, if using, and serve.

COCINAR CON AMOR: DISHES TO CELEBRATE

I am happiest when I'm at home, surrounded by friends and family, and cooking for them—after all, cooking is all about making people happy. These are the recipes that I turn to when I want to chill out, relax, and just enjoy.

Pastas, soups, slow-cooked meats, and rich, layered sauces are the dishes that comforted me the most when I was growing up, and these are the recipes I still turn to when I cook for the most important people in my life. Italian culture is a big part of life in Venezuela, from the name of our country (the word *Venezuela* comes from Venezia, or Venice) to the architecture and the food. I remember watching my best friend's Italian mom make classic Italian tomato sauce, packing enough away in glass jars to last the whole year.

When people are so hungry that they're banging their knives and forks on the table, I'll focus on fast dishes that use shortcuts like sofrito as a flavor base and high heat to caramelize the meats and vegetables, creating deep flavors in a quick way. On the other hand, if I have an afternoon or a whole day, I turn to ragùs and deep-flavored sauces that need time. I'll check on them every now and then, anticipating the end of the day when we'll indulge big time!

Cooking is a way of showing my love to the people whom I care for the most. It's how I was raised and how I like to nurture anyone that comes to my table.

CHEESY TELITAS FLATBREAD

Makes 8 telitas

1 cup Harina P.A.N. or masarepa corn flour

1 cup queso fresco

½ cup grated Parmigiano-Reggiano cheese

1 tablespoon finely chopped fresh basil

1 tablespoon extra-virgin olive oil plus more for shaping, if needed

¾ teaspoon kosher salt

Pinch of freshly ground black pepper

My mother used to make these cheese-stuffed flatbreads for me when I was a little girl in Venezuela. She'd come to my bedroom and gently whisper "telitas," and I knew that a fresh-griddled stack of them would be waiting for me on the table. Thicker than a tortilla but thinner than an arepa, a telita is crisp and golden on the outside and gives in to a melted string cheesy–like filling. The name comes from the word *tela*, meaning a piece of cloth (there is also a type of Latin cheese called telita, which is very soft, mild, and tasty). Telitas are very quick to make, meaning you can have them on your plate, from start to finish, in under twenty minutes. They're so versatile and are great served any time of day as a snack or a side (like a tortilla). Try them with Smashed Guacamole (page 100) or Carne Mechada (page 162). Harina P.A.N. or masarepa corn flour and queso fresco can be found in Latin markets and some supermarkets. See pages xiii–xix for more about these Latin ingredients.

1. Place the corn flour, queso fresco, Parmigiano-Reggiano cheese, basil, 1 tablespoon of the olive oil, the salt, and pepper in a large bowl and stir to combine. Pour ¾ cup of water over the mixture and use a wooden spoon to mix the ingredients until they come together into a rough dough ball.

2. Move the dough to a cutting board and knead for about 10 minutes, until it isn't sticky anymore and is very malleable, like Play-Doh.

3. Divide the dough into 8 equal pieces and roll each piece into a ball. Place a 14-inch-long sheet of plastic wrap on the work surface and lightly coat the entire sheet with nonstick

continued

vegetable cooking spray. Set a dough ball on the lower half of the sheet and fold the top half of the plastic over the dough. Using a tortilla press, a rolling pin, or your hands, press the dough ball into a 1/8-inch-thick disk, which is the telita. Remove the plastic wrap, place the dough disk on a lightly oiled baking sheet, and set aside. Reuse the plastic wrap (regreasing when necessary) to shape the remaining 7 dough balls.

4. Heat a medium skillet over medium-high heat. Slide a spatula under a telita and flip it into the hot pan. Cook the disk until it is browned and crispy, 3 to 4 minutes. Flip it over and brown the other side, 3 to 4 minutes longer. Place the telita on a plate and repeat with the remaining dough disks, stacking each on top of the other. Serve warm as a whole piece or sliced into quarters.

VARIATION: *Prosciutto Telitas Pizza*

After cooking a telita on one side, flip it and spread 1 1/2 teaspoons mascarpone-basil spread (see recipe notes, page 133) on the browned side. Place a slice of tomato on top, followed by a slice of prosciutto and 1 tablespoon grated Parmigiano-Reggiano cheese on top. Immediately remove the pizza from the pan, place it on a plate, and serve.

PROSCIUTTO *and* CILANTRO-RICOTTA SPREAD *on* BREAD

Serves 4

1 cup loosely packed fresh cilantro leaves

1 cup ricotta cheese

Pinch of kosher salt

Pinch of freshly ground black pepper

1 baguette, thinly sliced on the diagonal into 16 pieces

16 slices prosciutto

Freezing tender, fresh herbs like basil and cilantro overnight before pulverizing them into a powder results in an intensity that takes this spread to the next level. Plus, it's a good way to preserve these fragile ingredients. Here the spread is topped with thinly sliced prosciutto for a more hearty bite, but you can leave it off for a meat-free option. You absolutely must try it spread between layers of still-warm telitas (see page 131). The ricotta melts like butter, and in turn the unbelievably vibrant taste of the cilantro comes out front and center. The spread can be made with fresh basil and mascarpone for a more Italian-inspired taste and can be refrigerated for up to one week.

1. Place the cilantro leaves on a paper towel and gently fold the paper towel over the herbs so it will fit in a resealable plastic freezer bag. Freeze the cilantro overnight.

2. Remove the cilantro from the freezer and place it in the bowl of a food processor. Add the ricotta, salt, and pepper. Process the mixture until it is smooth. Scrape the mixture into an airtight container and refrigerate until using.

3. Spread a little of the cilantro-ricotta mixture onto each piece of bread. Drape with a slice of prosciutto and serve.

SPICY GINGER *and* ORANGE-GLAZED CHICKEN WINGS

Serves 6

- ½ cup fresh orange juice
- ¼ cup hoisin sauce
- 3 tablespoons fresh lemon juice (from 1 lemon)
- 1 tablespoon canola oil
- ¼ cup sugar
- 3 garlic cloves, very finely minced
- One 2-inch piece fresh ginger, peeled and very finely chopped (about 2 tablespoons)
- 2 pounds chicken wings
- 3 scallions, white and light green parts only, thinly sliced

Easy, juicy, and gingery chicken wings are just the thing for entertaining a crowd. A sprinkle of fresh scallions just before serving gives the wings a welcome freshness and sharp flavor. These are best served as an appetizer or alongside other finger foods like Smashed Guacamole (page 100) and empanaditas (see pages 33 and 35). Note that the wings need to marinate overnight or up to three days to reach their maximum flavor potential. You can also marinate them and then freeze them in a gallon-size resealable plastic freezer bag: Thaw completely in the refrigerator and they're ready for roasting.

1. Pour the orange juice, hoisin sauce, lemon juice, and canola oil into a gallon-size resealable plastic bag. Add the sugar, garlic, and ginger. Seal and vigorously shake to combine. Add the chicken wings and turn to coat in the marinade. Seal the bag and refrigerate overnight or up to 3 days.

2. Preheat the oven to 400°F. Line a rimmed baking sheet with aluminum foil.

3. Remove the wings from the bag and place them on the baking sheet. Roast the wings until deep golden brown and shiny, about 45 minutes. Remove them from the oven and let cool for 5 minutes. Transfer the chicken wings to a serving platter, sprinkle with the scallions, and serve.

LENTIL, POTATO, *and* BACON SOUP

Serves 6

8 to 10 cups Beef Stock (page 210) or store-bought beef broth

2 cups brown lentils, rinsed and drained

4 bacon slices, finely chopped

1 cup Basic Sofrito (page 202)

1 small Yukon gold potato, peeled and finely chopped

1 tablespoon ground cumin

1½ teaspoons garlic powder

1 bay leaf

½ cup finely chopped fresh cilantro

½ cup finely chopped fresh flat-leaf parsley

¼ cup finely chopped fresh thyme

2 tablespoons extra-virgin olive oil

1 tablespoon kosher salt

1 teaspoon freshly ground black pepper

When it comes to Latin side dishes, everyone automatically envisions black or red beans ladled over a dish of fluffy, steamed white rice. But in Argentina and Venezuela, lentils are served just as often as black and red beans either as a side dish or as a satisfying soup. Whether the soup is thin and brothy or thick and stewy, lentils deliver a high-protein, healthy meal at a very low cost. You can serve the soup as is, cook it longer for a thicker, chunkier stew-style soup, or blend all or some of it for a creamier consistency.

1. Bring the beef stock to a boil in a large soup pot. Add the lentils and boil for 3 minutes. Reduce the heat to medium-low and simmer until they are al dente, about 45 minutes.

2. Meanwhile, place the bacon in a large skillet over medium-high heat. Cook, stirring occasionally, until the bacon is just starting to get crispy, 3 to 5 minutes. Reduce the heat to low, stir in the sofrito, potatoes, cumin, garlic powder, and bay leaf and cook until the potatoes start to soften around the edges, about 5 minutes. Remove and discard the bay leaf. Scrape the sofrito mixture into the pot with the lentils.

3. Stir in the cilantro, parsley, thyme, olive oil, salt, and pepper and cook until the lentils are very soft but are still holding their shape, about 15 minutes. Divide the soup among six bowls and serve immediately.

CHICKEN *and* RICE CHUPE

Serves 6

2 pounds bone-in chicken breasts or thighs

4 tablespoons fresh lemon juice (from about 1¹/₂ lemons)

1 tablespoon kosher salt

1 teaspoon freshly ground black pepper

2 tablespoons extra-virgin olive oil

8 cups Chicken Stock (page 211) or store-bought chicken broth

2 leeks, white and light green parts only, trimmed, halved, and thinly sliced

1 red potato, peeled and cut into ¹/₂-inch cubes

1 carrot, chopped into ¹/₂-inch pieces

1¹/₄ cups long-grain white rice

¹/₂ cup roughly chopped fresh cilantro, plus 2 tablespoons whole leaves for serving

A chupe is a chunky, chowder-style soup typically found in Peru (the name stems from the Italian *cioppino*, a soup similar to bouillabaisse). My mom's method for making chicken chupe was to fill a pot with tons of vegetables and chicken and let it bubble away on the stove for an entire day. The idea was that the soup would deliver all of the flavors and nutrients of the vegetables and meats she put into it. She'd serve the broth separately from the chicken and vegetables, with lots of add-ins on the side: white rice, avocados, chopped cilantro, jalapeños, arepas, even a small pitcher of cream to make the broth richer. To this day, when my family gets together in Miami, this is what she makes. My simplified version is a lot quicker than Mom's and more like a broth than a chowder. It gets a fantastic boost of flavor from the liquefied cilantro and fresh lemon juice that get stirred in at the end.

1. Place the chicken pieces in a large bowl. Pour 3 tablespoons of the lemon juice over the chicken, season with the salt and pepper, and set aside.

2. Heat the olive oil in a large pot over medium-high heat. Add the chicken skin side down and cook until it's golden, about 5 minutes. Pour the chicken stock over the chicken and bring to a boil. Reduce the heat to medium-low and simmer until the chicken is cooked through, about 20 minutes.

3. Add the leeks, potatoes, and carrots to the pot and cook just until the leeks start to soften, about 5 minutes. Increase the heat to medium, add the rice, and cook until the rice is tender, about 20 minutes longer. Turn off the heat and set aside to cool for 20 minutes.

continued

4. Remove the chicken from the soup and place it on a cutting board. Pull the meat away from the bones, discard the bones, and use your fingers to shred the meat. Return the chicken to the pot and heat the soup over medium-high heat. Add the remaining 1 tablespoon lemon juice and turn off the heat.

5. Place the chopped cilantro in the bowl of a food processor or a blender jar along with 1/2 cup of the soup broth and puree until smooth. Stir the liquefied cilantro into the chicken soup and divide the soup among six bowls. Place a few cilantro leaves on top and serve.

VARIATION: *Chicken Chupe with Masa Dumplings*

Make the soup following the recipe above, omitting the rice. While the leeks, potatoes, and carrots are cooking, make a half batch of the arepa dough as instructed on page 30. Roll marble-size pieces of dough into balls and add them to the simmering soup (before you add the remaining 1 tablespoon lemon juice). Once the dough balls rise to the top, simmer them until they're cooked through, about 15 minutes. Add the lemon juice and liquefied cilantro and serve.

CRUZADO

3 quarts Beef Stock (page 210) or store-bought beef broth

2 carrots, rougly chopped

2 celery stalks, roughly chopped

1 large yellow onion, roughly chopped

2 pounds boneless beef shanks or stew meat, cut into 2-inch pieces

2 pounds bone-in chicken thighs, skin removed

3 Yukon gold potatoes, peeled and cut into 1-inch cubes

2 ears of corn, husked and sliced crosswise into 1-inch wheels

1 parsnip, peeled and roughly chopped

1/2 pound butternut squash, cut into 1-inch cubes (about 1 cup)

1 semiripe (yellow with a few black spots on the skin) plantain, peeled and cut into 1/2-inch cubes

1 yucca, peeled and cut into 1/2-inch cubes

1/3 cup finely chopped fresh cilantro

1/3 cup finely chopped fresh mint

1/3 cup finely chopped fresh flat-leaf parsley

1 tablespoon kosher salt

6 large green cabbage leaves

Basic White Rice (page 204) or Venezuelan Arepas (page 30) for serving

Hot sauce (optional)

1 Hass avocado, halved, pitted, peeled, and chopped (optional)

3 ounces queso fresco, cut into small cubes (about 3/4 cup; optional)

1 lime, cut into 6 wedges

Cruzado means crossed—referring to the cross section of vegetables and meats that are in it—and this soup literally seems like a hodgepodge of every stick-to-your-bones root vegetable, along with hearty beef shanks and chicken thighs for good measure. Traditionally the meat and vegetables are served in one bowl, and the strained broth is ladled into another. So from one pot of soup, you get two. The soup is excellent served with a bowl of Basic White Rice (page 204) or a stack of hot, fresh-baked Venezuelan arepas (page 30) on the side, and some diced avocado and semifirm cheese like queso fresco, a dash of hot sauce, and lime wedges for garnish.

1. Pour the beef stock into a large pot. Add the carrots, celery, and onions and bring the mixture to a boil over high heat. Gently drop the beef shanks into the pot, reduce the heat to low, and gently simmer for 30 minutes.

2. Add the chicken, potatoes, corn, parsnips, and butternut squash and cook for 20 minutes.

3. Stir in the plantains, yucca, cilantro, mint, and parsley and cook until the vegetables and meat are very tender, about 1 hour.

4. Stir in the salt and then lay the cabbage leaves over the soup, overlapping them to cover the surface completely. Cover the pot with a lid and cook for 5 minutes, then turn off the heat and let the soup stand for 20 minutes.

5. To serve, place the rice or arepas and the hot sauce, if using, on the table. Place the avocados and quesa fresco, if using, in separate bowls and set alongside the rice or arepas. Use tongs to remove the cabbage leaves and place them in a

continued

large bowl or on a platter. Divide the soup into bowls or serve it like we do in South America by removing the meat and vegetables and placing them in a bowl or on a platter and straining the broth through a fine-mesh sieve into a soup tureen or large pot. Serve alongside garnishes like rice, hot sauce, avocado, queso fresco, and lime wedges.

Sabes Qué?

Give store-bought salsa a fresh edge by adding a splash of white vinegar, a chopped jalapeño or Serrano chile, a finely chopped or thinly sliced small red or white onion, one or two finely minced garlic cloves, and a handful of chopped cilantro. Give it a stir, place the lid back on, and refrigerate until needed. The salsa is best if eaten within a few weeks, but I've had jars for up to two months in the fridge!

SKIRT STEAK RAGÙ

Serves 8

1 tablespoon extra-virgin olive oil

2½ pounds skirt steak, silverskin and excess fat removed, sliced into 4-inch pieces

12 garlic cloves, very finely minced

2 carrots, halved crosswise

2 celery stalks, halved crosswise

1 yellow onion, halved

1 shallot, very finely chopped

8 cups Tomato Sauce (page 207) or store-bought tomato sauce, strained through a fine-mesh sieve

2 cups dry red wine (such as cabernet sauvignon or merlot)

1 cup Beef Stock (page 210) or Chicken Stock (page 211) or store-bought beef or chicken broth

2 tablespoons agave syrup

1 bunch fresh basil leaves

1 tablespoon plus 1 teaspoon kosher salt

½ teaspoon freshly ground black pepper

1 pound penne or rigatoni

Grated Parmigiano-Reggiano cheese for serving

Traveling is a huge part of my life. I get so inspired by different places, people, and cuisines that I try to re-create these memories in the kitchen once I return home. One of my favorite places to visit is Italy because my very best friend, who I grew up with in Caracas, lives there. The last time I visited, I walked through the front door and there was Nella, at the stove, stirring a big beautiful pot of ragù, just like a typical Italian mama. The smell was incredible, and the ragù tasted even better, bursting with the flavor of sun-ripened tomatoes from her garden. Here I use imported Italian bottled strained tomato sauce because I feel it most closely replicates the flavor of tomatoes in Italy. It's a little pricey, but it's a lot cheaper than a plane ticket!

1. Heat the olive oil in a large pot over high heat. Add the steak and cook until browned on each side, 8 to 10 minutes total. Stir in the garlic, carrots, celery, onion, and shallots. Pour in the tomato sauce, red wine, stock, and agave syrup. Add the basil, 1 teaspoon of the salt, and the pepper and bring everything to a boil. Reduce the heat to medium-low, cover the pot so the lid sits askew, and cook until the meat pulls apart when gently prodded with a fork, about 4 hours, stirring every 20 minutes.

2. Bring a large pot of water to a boil. Add the remaining 1 tablespoon salt and the penne and cook following the package instructions until it is al dente. Drain and add the pasta to the pot with the sauce. Use tongs to toss together, sprinkle with Parmigiano-Reggiano cheese, and serve.

QUINOA, SWEET PEPPERS, *and* FIG SALAD

Serves 4

1 cup dry sherry

½ cup dried currants

1 cup quinoa

2½ cups Chicken Stock (page 211) or store-bought chicken broth

2 scallions, white and light green parts only, thinly sliced

1 cup fresh figs, stemmed and chopped

1 carrot, finely chopped

¼ green bell pepper, finely chopped

¼ red bell pepper, finely chopped

¼ yellow bell pepper, finely chopped

¼ cup finely chopped fresh cilantro

⅓ cup Tangy Citrus Vinaigrette (page 74)

Quinoa, a native South American grain, has a wonderfully fluffy texture that tastes nutty and sweet with a bite somewhere between couscous and brown rice. Here its earthy flavor is enhanced with sweet figs and dried currants. The currants get softened in sherry first, so they become buttery and musky. The citrus vinaigrette gives the salad a brightness and punch.

1. Pour the sherry into a medium bowl. Add the currants and set aside to rehydrate for 20 minutes. Drain the currants, discard any remaining sherry, and set the currants aside.

2. Place the quinoa in a fine-mesh sieve and rinse under cold running water. Bring the chicken stock to a boil in a medium saucepan over high heat. Add the quinoa and return to a boil. Cover, reduce the heat to low, and cook until the quinoa is tender, 20 to 25 minutes. Scrape the quinoa into a large bowl and set aside to cool.

3. Stir the scallions, figs, carrots, bell peppers, and cilantro into the cooled quinoa. Pour the citrus vinaigrette over the salad and stir gently to combine. Serve immediately or refrigerate for up to 3 days. The salad can be served cold or at room temperature.

CREAMY LEMON BOW TIES *with* SHRIMP

Serves 4

1 pound farfalle (bow tie) pasta

2 tablespoons extra-virgin olive oil

6 garlic cloves, very finely minced

2 shallots, very finely chopped

1½ pounds large shrimp, peeled, deveined, and halved lengthwise

1 teaspoon kosher salt

Zest and juice of 1 lemon

¼ cup Chicken Stock (page 211) or store-bought chicken broth

¼ cup dry white wine (such as pinot grigio)

2½ cups heavy cream

1½ cups grated Parmigiano-Reggiano cheese, plus extra for serving

1 tablespoon finely chopped fresh flat-leaf parsley

¼ cup finely chopped fresh tomatoes for serving (optional)

High heat brings out the pungency of the garlic and shallots and caramelizes the shrimp in this decadent alfredo-style pasta dish. Lemon juice and white wine bring fresh, savory qualities while a touch of cream and Parmigiano-Reggiano cheese give it that wonderfully rich creaminess for which alfredo sauce is famous.

1. Bring a large pot of salted water to a boil. Add the farfalle and cook according to the package instructions until it is al dente. Drain, return to the pot, and set aside.

2. Heat the olive oil, garlic, and shallots in a large skillet, over high heat, stirring often, until the garlic is fragrant, about 30 seconds. Add the shrimp and salt, stirring the shrimp just until they begin to turn pink, about 2 minutes. Use tongs to transfer the shrimp to a large bowl and set aside. Try to leave as much of the shallots and garlic in the skillet as possible.

3. Add the lemon zest, lemon juice, chicken stock, and white wine to the skillet and bring to a boil. Reduce the heat to medium-high and simmer until the liquid is reduced by half. Stir the cream into the simmering broth and cook until it thickens, 8 to 10 minutes. Whisk in the grated Parmigiano-Reggiano cheese until it is completely melted. Continue to stir over high heat until the sauce thickens slightly, about 5 minutes.

4. Return the shrimp to the skillet and cook for a minute. Turn off the heat and toss ½ cup of the sauce with the pasta and then divide the pasta and among four plates. Divide the remaining sauce evenly over each plate of pasta, sprinkle with Parmigiano-Reggiano cheese, parsley, and tomatoes (if using), and serve.

SEAFOOD BOLOGNESE

Serves 6

2 tablespoons extra-virgin olive oil

6 ounces 1/8-inch-thick calamari rings

6 garlic cloves, very finely minced

1 large shallot, very finely minced

3 cups (about 1 pound) fresh or canned lump crabmeat

6 ounces skinless salmon fillets, sliced into 1/2-inch cubes

1/4 cup dry white wine (such as pinot grigio)

3 1/2 cups Tomato Sauce (page 207) or store-bought tomato sauce

1 cup Chicken Stock (page 211) or store-bought chicken broth

1/4 cup dry sherry

1 pound whole wheat linguine

1 tablespoon plus 1/2 teaspoon kosher salt

2 teaspoons crushed red pepper flakes

2 teaspoons sugar

2 tablespoons unsalted butter

1/2 cup quartered cherry tomatoes

1/4 cup grated Parmigiano-Reggiano cheese, plus extra for serving

1/4 cup finely chopped fresh flat-leaf parsley

2 tablespoons brine-packed capers, rinsed

1/4 teaspoon freshly ground black pepper

2 tablespoons finely chopped fresh basil

Made with the winning combination of calamari, crab, and salmon, this satisfying meatless bolognese pasta dish never leaves you feeling heavy and weighed down, making it versatile enough to be served at any time of the year. What's really excellent about the bolognese is that you can keep the calamari and salmon handy in the freezer and a large can of crab in the pantry, making this dish great for drop-in company (which, coincidentally, is how I created the recipe).

1. Heat the olive oil in a large pot over high heat. Add the calamari, cook for 1 minute (without stirring), and then stir in the garlic and shallots. Once the garlic is fragrant, after about 1 minute, add the crabmeat and salmon, cooking until the salmon is browned, 1 to 2 minutes. Turn the salmon over to brown the other side, 1 to 2 minutes longer (it's okay if some of the salmon flakes apart when you turn it—it just becomes a part of the sauce).

2. Pour in the white wine, bring to a simmer, and cook until it is slightly reduced, about 2 minutes. Pour in the tomato sauce and bring to a simmer, using a wooden spoon to gently stir the seafood (you don't want to break up the salmon too much) and cooking for 1 minute. Add the chicken stock and sherry, bring to a simmer, and cook for 4 minutes. Reduce the heat to medium-low and gently simmer the sauce until it is slightly thickened, about 20 minutes.

3. Meanwhile, bring a large pot of water to a boil. Add the linguine and 1 tablespoon of the salt and cook according to the package instructions until the pasta is al dente. Drain and set aside.

continued

4. Stir the red pepper flakes and sugar into the seafood sauce and then add the butter, cherry tomatoes, Parmigiano-Reggiano cheese, parsley, capers, the remaining ½ teaspoon salt, and the black pepper. Cook to bring the flavors together, about 5 minutes longer, and then stir in the drained pasta, gently tossing it with the sauce. Divide the pasta among six bowls, sprinkle with Parmigiano-Reggiano cheese and basil, and serve immediately.

Sabes Qué?

To quickly defrost frozen fish, place it in a colander and under cold, running water (about 10 minutes for a thin fillet). For thick fillets, fill a large bowl with cold water and submerge the fillet for about 20 minutes to thaw (discard warmed water and replenish with more cold water as needed).

CHICKEN ALBONDIGAS
with LEMON PICCATA SAUCE

Serves 4

FOR THE MEATBALLS

- 1 pound ground chicken
- 1/2 cup dried bread crumbs, preferably made from brioche or challah bread
- 1/4 cup low-fat plain Greek yogurt
- 1/4 cup finely chopped fresh cilantro
- 1/4 cup finely chopped fresh flat-leaf parsley
- 2 tablespoons finely chopped fresh thyme
- 3 garlic cloves, very finely minced
- 1 shallot, very finely minced
- 1/2 teaspoon ground ginger
- 1 1/2 teaspoons kosher salt
- 1 teaspoon freshly ground black pepper
- 2 tablespoons extra-virgin olive oil

FOR THE SAUCE

- 1 tablespoon extra-virgin olive oil
- 1/3 cup plus 1 1/2 tablespoons brine-packed capers, rinsed
- 6 garlic cloves, very finely minced
- 1 shallot, finely minced
- 3 tablespoons Basic Sofrito (page 202)
- 1 teaspoon kosher salt
- 1/2 teaspoon freshly ground black pepper
- 2 cups Chicken Stock (page 211) or store-bought chicken broth
  Juice of 2 lemons
- 1 tablespoon ground arrowroot
- 2 tablespoons unsalted butter

There are a lot of different approaches to *albondigas*, Latin-style meatballs. The ones featured here infuse ground chicken with lots of fresh cilantro, thyme, and parsley for a bright herb taste; adding yogurt to the mixture makes for a light texture. The meatballs get topped with a piquant citrus-caper sauce—I keep the flavor sharp by using quick-working arrowroot to thicken the sauce without losing its bright flavor (cornstarch needs to be simmered until it thickens, thereby cooking out some of the freshness of the citrus and herbs). While I'm definitely stepping away from Latin tradition here, I still use a sofrito base for the sauce, which is truly the key to developing big flavor fast. Sophisticated and elegant, the meatballs are especially good for parties (serve them individually on bamboo skewers).

1. Place the ground chicken in a colander and set it in a large bowl or in the sink. Let the chicken drain while assembling the ingredients for the meatballs and sauce.

2. To make the meatballs, place the bread crumbs, yogurt, cilantro, parsley, thyme, garlic, shallot, ginger, salt, and pepper in a large bowl and stir to combine. Add the ground chicken and mix well. Scrape the chicken mixture out onto a large sheet of plastic wrap, fold the plastic over the chicken to seal, and refrigerate for 30 minutes.

3. Remove the chicken mixture from the refrigerator and divide and shape it into 12 balls. Heat the olive oil in a large skillet over medium-high heat. Add the meatballs and cook on all sides until golden brown, about 7 minutes (they won't be cooked all the way through). Transfer the meatballs to a paper towel–lined plate or rimmed baking sheet and set aside.

continued

4. To make the sauce, heat the olive oil in a large pot over medium-high heat. Add the capers, garlic, shallots, sofrito, salt, and pepper and cook, stirring often, until the shallots begin to brown, about 3 minutes. Pour in the chicken stock and lemon juice and bring to a boil. Reduce the heat to medium and simmer until slightly reduced, about 3 minutes.

5. Place the arrowroot in a small bowl, add 2 tablespoons of water, and stir until the arrowroot is dissolved. Set aside.

6. Place the meatballs in the sauce, reduce the heat to medium-low, cover, and cook until the meatballs are cooked through and firm to the touch, about 20 minutes longer. Stir in the butter, and once it is melted, stir in the arrowroot mixture and cook until the sauce has thickened and become glossy, about 3 minutes. Divide the meatballs and their sauce among four bowls and serve.

Sabes Qué?

Freshly made bread crumbs are delicious, easy, and economical. Dry a few slices of bread on a countertop overnight (place the bread on a wire rack so both sides dry out evenly) and then pulse in a food processor until the crumbs are the texture you like. Or, dry bread slices in a 300°F oven (again, place them on a wire rack so the bread dries evenly) until dry and crisp, about 30 minutes. Remove from the oven and set aside to cool, then pulse in a food processor until fine.

CREAMY RIGATONI *with* CHICKEN *and* PORTABELLAS

Serves 6

- 2 tablespoons extra-virgin olive oil
- 1 shallot, very finely minced
- 2 garlic cloves, very finely minced
- 1½ pounds boneless, skinless chicken breasts, cut into 1-inch cubes
- 2 portabella mushrooms, stemmed and cut into 1-inch cubes
- 2 tomatoes, peeled, seeded, and diced
- 1 cup tomato puree (preferably bottled Italian tomato puree), strained through a fine-mesh sieve
- 2 cups heavy cream
- ½ cup dry white wine (such as pinot grigio)
- ¼ cup Chicken Stock (page 211) or store-bought chicken broth
- 1 teaspoon kosher salt
- ½ teaspoon freshly ground black pepper
- 2 cups grated Parmigiano-Reggiano cheese, plus extra for serving
- 1 pound rigatoni
- 1 tablespoon finely chopped fresh flat-leaf parsley

This is my family's absolute favorite pasta dish and has been for more than a decade. It was featured on the menu at my first Miami restaurant, Food Café, where my nephew Carlos would come into the kitchen, order a double-portion, top it with a churrasco steak, and dig in. He still comes into my home kitchen and demands, "Pasta Food, *Tía!*" He is like a son to me ... who am I to refuse?

1. Heat the olive oil in a large pot over medium-high heat. Add the shallots and cook, stirring often, until they begin to brown, about 1 minute. Stir in the garlic and chicken and cook until the chicken is browned, about 6 minutes. Use tongs to turn over the chicken pieces, and cook the other side until browned, about 5 minutes longer. Stir in the mushrooms and cook for 1 minute, then add the tomatoes, tomato puree, cream, white wine, chicken stock, salt, and pepper. Bring to a boil, reduce the heat to medium-low, and cook until the sauce is thick and reduced by half, about 10 minutes.

2. Stir in the Parmigiano-Reggiano cheese and cook, stirring often, until the sauce is thick, about 10 minutes.

3. While the sauce simmers, bring a large pot of salted water to a boil. Add the rigatoni and cook following the package instructions until the pasta is al dente. Drain and return to the pot. Add 1 cup of the sauce to the pasta and toss to coat. Divide the pasta among six bowls, divide the remaining sauce evenly over each bowl of pasta, sprinkle with some Parmigiano-Reggiano cheese and parsley, and serve.

PASTA PICADILLO

Serves 8

- 2 tablespoons extra-virgin olive oil
- 2 pounds lean ground beef
- 1 pound ground veal
- 1 pound ground pork
- 12 garlic cloves, very finely minced
- 3 celery stalks, finely chopped
- 2 carrots, finely chopped
- 2 medium yellow onions, finely chopped
- 2 shallots, very finely chopped
- 12 large basil leaves, stacked, tightly rolled, and thinly sliced crosswise, plus extra for serving
- One 12-ounce can whole peeled tomatoes with juice, crushed by hand
- 3 cups Tomato Sauce (page 207) or store-bought tomato sauce
- 3 cups Beef Stock (page 210) or store-bought beef broth
- 1 cup dry red wine (such as cabernet sauvignon or merlot)
- 1 tablespoon sugar
- 1 teaspoon dried thyme
- 1/2 teaspoon ground cumin
- 1/2 teaspoon sweet paprika
- 1 teaspoon kosher salt
- 1/2 teaspoon freshly ground black pepper
- 1 pound linguine, rigatoni, or spaghetti
- 2 tablespoons unsalted butter
- Grated Parmigiano-Reggiano cheese for serving

Picadillo in Spanish means that everything is chopped very small, and such is the case in this pasta with picadillo meat sauce, my Latin take on the traditional Italian bolognese. In Venezuela and much of South America, picadillo is a very well known and versatile dish of ground beef, tomatoes, peppers, chiles, and onions. We eat it with rice, with a fried egg, as a side dish, and even use it as a filling for empanadas, which is what my mom did. She'd make the best empanadas in the world using leftover picadillo from the night before. I either follow her lead and make picadillo empanaditas or turn leftovers into a Latin shepherd's pie by spreading the leftover picadillo sauce into a baking dish and topping it with mashed sweet plantains.

1. Heat the olive oil in a large heavy-bottomed pot over high heat. Add the ground beef, ground veal, and ground pork and cook, stirring often to break up the meat, until the meat is browned and the liquid begins to evaporate, about 20 minutes.

2. Stir in the garlic, celery, carrots, onions, shallots, and basil and cook until the onions and celery are soft, about 10 minutes. Add the crushed tomatoes, tomato sauce, 2 3/4 cups of the beef stock, the red wine, sugar, thyme, cumin, paprika, salt, and pepper. Bring to a boil, cook for 1 minute, and then reduce the heat to medium-low. Cover the pot so the lid rests slightly askew and continue to simmer until the sauce becomes a semithick, medium brown sauce, about 3 hours.

3. Bring a large pot of salted water to a boil. Cook the pasta according to the package instructions until it is al dente. Drain and return to the pot. Add the remaining 1/4 cup beef stock and the butter. Once the butter is melted, transfer the pasta to a large serving dish. Ladle the sauce over the top and finish with a sprinkle of Parmigiano-Reggiano cheese and basil.

POLLO CON PASSION

Serves 4

1 tablespoon grated orange zest plus 1/2 cup fresh orange juice (from about 2 oranges)

1/4 cup passion fruit juice

1/4 cup soy sauce

2 tablespoons agave syrup

2 tablespoons champagne vinegar

1 tablespoon ketchup

1 tablespoon tomato paste

1 tablespoon lemon zest (from about 3 lemons)

1 teaspoon garlic powder

1 teaspoon onion powder

1/2 teaspoon Worcestershire sauce

3 baking potatoes, peeled and quartered

1 yellow onion, quartered and sliced crosswise

1 carrot, finely chopped

1 celery stalk, finely chopped

One 3 1/2- to 4-pound chicken, cut into 8 pieces

1 teaspoon kosher salt

1 teaspoon freshly ground black pepper

For big family meals and nearly any birthday party we ever celebrated at my home in Venezuela, my nanny Leo would make her famous sweet-sour passion fruit roasted chicken and vegetables. Leo used orange juice, passion fruit juice, and soy sauce as the base for the sauce, which she'd just pour right over the chicken before it baked on top of potatoes, onions, carrots, and celery. Everything roasted together in the oven, creating a wonderfully deep-flavored chicken dinner that I still crave to this day.

1. Preheat the oven to 400°F.

2. Whisk together the orange juice, orange zest, passion fruit juice, soy sauce, agave syrup, vinegar, ketchup, tomato paste, lemon zest, garlic powder, onion powder, and Worcestershire sauce in a medium bowl and set aside.

3. Place the potatoes, onions, carrots, and celery in the bottom of a roasting pan, tossing with your hands to combine. Set the chicken pieces on top of the vegetables and then season the chicken and vegetables with the salt and pepper. Pour the orange–passion fruit sauce over the chicken and vegetables and turn them to coat. Rearrange the chicken so it is skin side up on top of the vegetables.

4. Cover the roasting pan with aluminum foil and roast the chicken for 30 minutes. Remove and discard the foil. Continue roasting the chicken until the skin is crisp and deep brown, about 1 hour longer. Remove the roasting pan from the oven, divide the chicken and vegetables among four plates, and serve.

CRISPY OVEN-FRIED CHICKEN
with COLLARDS

Serves 4

FOR THE CHICKEN

- **4** skinless, bone-in chicken breasts, halved, or 8 skinless drumsticks
- **1** teaspoon kosher salt
- **1/2** teaspoon freshly ground black pepper
- **4** cups cornflakes, lightly crushed
- **1 1/2** tablespoons garlic powder
- **1 1/2** tablespoons onion powder
- **1** teaspoon ground ginger
- **1** teaspoon crushed red pepper flakes (optional)
- **1** teaspoon poultry seasoning
- **2** cups buttermilk or nonfat milk
- **1** tablespoon vegetable oil
  Few pinches of sweet paprika

FOR THE GREENS

- **2** tablespoons extra-virgin olive oil
- **6** garlic cloves, very finely minced
- **2** pounds collard greens, thick stems removed, leaves stacked, rolled, and thinly sliced crosswise
- **1** tablespoon finely chopped fresh flat-leaf parsley
- **1** tablespoon finely chopped fresh cilantro
- **1** teaspoon kosher salt
- **1** teaspoon freshly ground black pepper

Collard greens are huge in South America and are a real staple of our cuisine. We eat them briefly pan-seared with lots of garlic and herbs, making them quite different from the long-stewed collards of the American South. They are a natural match to oven-fried chicken. The cornflakes make the crust extra crisp. You can make the fried chicken kid-friendly by using boneless chicken tenders. Take it one step further and get the kids involved by inviting them to shake the chicken in the bag themselves!

1. Rinse the chicken under cold running water and pat it dry. Place it on a rimmed baking sheet or large plate, season with the salt and black pepper, and set aside.

2. Place the cornflake crumbs in a gallon-size resealable plastic bag. Add the garlic powder, onion powder, ginger, red pepper flakes, if using, and 1/2 teaspoon of the poultry seasoning. Seal the bag and shake to combine. Pour the buttermilk into a large bowl, whisk in the remaining 1/2 teaspoon poultry seasoning, and add the chicken pieces, tossing them with the liquid to coat. Add one piece of chicken to the cornflake mixture at a time, sealing the bag and shaking it to evenly coat the chicken. Remove the chicken from the bag and return it to the baking sheet. Repeat with the remaining chicken pieces. Refrigerate the chicken on the baking sheet for 1 hour.

3. Preheat the oven to 350°F.

4. Remove the baking sheet from the refrigerator. Place the chicken on a large plate and grease the baking sheet with the vegetable oil. Return the chicken to the baking sheet, sprinkle it with the paprika, cover the baking sheet with aluminum foil, and bake the chicken for 40 minutes.

5. Remove the baking sheet from the oven and discard the

foil. Return the chicken to the oven and continue baking until the crust is crisp and the chicken meat easily falls away from the bone, 30 to 40 minutes longer.

6. While the chicken bakes, make the collards. Heat the olive oil in a large skillet over high heat. Add the garlic and cook until fragrant, stirring often, for about 1 minute. Add the collards to the skillet and toss with tongs to evenly coat in the oil and garlic. Cook, stirring occasionally, until they slightly wilt, about 5 minutes. Turn off the heat and add the parsley, cilantro, salt, and black pepper, tossing with tongs to combine.

7. Remove the chicken from the oven and cool for 5 minutes before serving with the collards on the side.

lighten up   After moving to the United States, I slowly started to gain weight. Adjusting to my new country also involved adjusting to the food, and like many people, I fell a little too much in love with fast food and big portions. Being in culinary school didn't exactly help me lose the extra pounds either—I was paying good money to learn, eat, and indulge all day long.

After I finished my culinary program, it became clear that in order to be a healthier person, I had to lose the extra pounds. Cooking is about control, and as a chef, I found it easy to lose the weight once I started paying attention to what was going into my body. There are no hidden calories or trans fats when you're cooking your own food. I watched my intake of carbohydrates and fat, ate my biggest meal at breakfast or lunch, and didn't eat after six o'clock in the evening. I continued to indulge—I'm a food lover first and foremost—I just indulged once or twice a week rather than once or twice a day.

Along the way, I learned how to modify dishes for a healthier outlook, like "fried" chicken (see page 159) that is oven-roasted for a lighter taste and a leaner nutritional profile, and the Seafood Bolognese (page 149) that is loaded with delicious and good-for-you salmon and calamari and no red meat at all. For me, cooking healthfully is about cooking with real ingredients that are satisfying and delicious.

CARNE MECHADA

Serves 6

2 pounds flank steak, extra fat removed

1 medium yellow onion, halved, and 1 small yellow onion, finely chopped

6 garlic cloves

1 red bell pepper, halved and seeded (leave one half whole; finely chop the other half)

½ cup whole cilantro sprigs

1 tablespoon plus 1 teaspoon kosher salt

2 tablespoons extra-virgin olive oil

½ small green bell pepper, seeded and finely chopped

1 shallot, very finely chopped

6 garlic cloves, very finely minced

1 tablespoon finely chopped fresh ají dulce or jarred pickled cherry peppers

2 tablespoons tomato paste

1 tablespoon Worcestershire sauce

2 bay leaves

2 teaspoons freshly ground black pepper

Basic White Rice (page 204) or Venezuelan Arepas (page 30) for serving

Made of simmered, shredded, and then pan-seared flank steak, this Venezuelan specialty is rich with garlic, bell peppers, and herbs and has an incredibly tender-hearty texture that makes it fantastic with rice, fried sweet plantains, and black beans, which is essentially the makeup of Venezuela's national dish, *pabellón criollo*. Carne mechada is very similar to Cuba's *ropa vieja*, but just a little less saucy, making it an excellent filling for arepitas (see page 32) or soft corn tortillas. It's also perfect served alongside sides like arepas and a few fried eggs.

1. Bring 12 cups of water to a boil in a large soup pot or stockpot. Add the steak, halved onion, garlic, red bell pepper half, cilantro sprigs, and 1 tablespoon of the salt and return to a boil. Reduce the heat to medium-low and simmer for 1 hour.

2. Strain the broth into a clean bowl. Set aside 2 cups for later and freeze the rest in a resealable plastic freezer bag to use another time (the broth can be stored in the freezer for up to 3 months). Set aside the meat to cool and discard the vegetables and cilantro. Once the meat is cool, use your fingers to shred it into long, thin strips. Set aside.

3. Heat the olive oil over high heat in a large, deep skillet or Dutch oven. Add the shredded meat to the pot and cook, stirring occasionally, until it has darkened and become slightly crisp around the edges, about 5 minutes. Add in the chopped onions, chopped red bell peppers, green bell peppers, shallots, garlic, ají dulce, and the remaining 1 teaspoon salt, cooking, stirring occasionally, until the onions and peppers begin

continued

to soften, about 5 minutes. Stir in the tomato paste and Worcestershire sauce, and add the reserved broth.

4.   Increase the heat to high and bring the mixture to a boil. Boil for 5 minutes, reduce the heat to medium, and stir in the bay leaves and black pepper. Simmer until the liquid reduces by half, 6 to 8 minutes. Remove and discard the bay leaves and serve with white rice or arepas.

VARIATION: *Arepitas Stuffed with Carne Mechada*

Split open the still-warm arepas like a pita pocket, making a slit in the top and wiggling a knife into the center of the arepa to create a pocket. Fill each arepa with about $1/2$ cup Carne Mechada (still hot for the best flavor) and serve right away.

CRANBERRY-CILANTRO BROWN RICE

Serves 4

1 cup long-grain brown rice

1 tablespoon kosher salt

2 tablespoons vegetable oil

½ shallot, very finely chopped

3 garlic cloves, very finely minced

¾ cup finely chopped fresh cilantro, plus a sprig for serving

½ cup dried cranberries

I make this stunning brown rice dish to add a healthy balance to a calorie-laden holiday spread. Cilantro and dried cranberries enhance the toasty, slightly chewy rice with their vivid green and red colors and wonderfully herby-sweet flavor. This is excellent alongside turkey, short ribs, roast chicken, or fish.

1. Bring 2 cups of water, the rice, and salt to a boil in a medium saucepan over high heat. Let the rice boil until some of the water is absorbed into the rice and the bubbles are popping close to the surface of the rice, about 4 minutes. Cover the pan, reduce the heat to low, and cook until all of the water is absorbed and the rice is slightly al dente, 25 to 30 minutes. Turn off the heat, uncover, use a fork to fluff the rice, and set aside for 10 minutes to cool.

2. Heat the vegetable oil in a medium skillet over medium-high heat. Add the shallots and garlic and cook while stirring until the garlic is fragrant, about 20 seconds. Stir in the rice, cilantro, and cranberries and turn out the rice into a bowl. Finish with a sprig of cilantro and serve.

Sabes Qué?

If you have leftover white or brown rice in the refrigerator, simply add it to the shallots and garlic and then stir in the cilantro and dried cranberries. You may want to add a few tablespoons of water to the pan and cover it to plump the rice before serving.

FRESH HERB SIDE SALAD

Serves 4

2 tablespoons extra-virgin olive oil

1 teaspoon fresh lemon juice

1 teaspoon kosher salt

1 teaspoon freshly ground black pepper

1/4 cup fresh celery leaves

1/4 cup fresh cilantro leaves

1/4 cup small fresh mint leaves

1/4 cup fresh flat-leaf parsley leaves

This simple whole herb side dish is an excellent accompaniment to meat dishes like Carne Mechada (page 162) or Crispy Oven-Fried Chicken with Collards (page 160). Splashed with good, fruity olive oil and spiked with a little lemon juice, it instantly lends a light feel to a meal—even if it is braised steak that you're eating. Celery leaves are at once unexpected and familiar, adding a wonderful soft celery flavor to the cilantro, mint, and parsley—simply pluck the tender leaves from the tops of the celery stalks. To serve this side salad as a more traditional salad course, double the dressing and add 2 cups of your favorite salad greens to the herbs.

1. Whisk together the olive oil, lemon juice, salt, and pepper in a small bowl.

2. Toss the celery leaves, cilantro leaves, mint leaves, and parsley leaves together in a medium bowl. Drizzle with the seasoned oil and serve.

SATISFYING THE BIGGEST SWEET TOOTH—MINE!

I am absolutely crazy for dessert. Chocolate, caramel, dulce de leche, fruit—you name it, I crave it. The desserts in this chapter are all about contrasts, like between the sharpness of goat cheese and a juicy grilled papaya or the creaminess of rum-spiked mascarpone and crunchy biscotti. I also play with temperature—literally (drizzling a hot golden chocolate sauce over fresh berries) and figuratively (adding jalapeño *and* cayenne pepper to chocolate mousse).

Some sweets are very Latin. I cannot imagine a Latin cookbook, *nuevo* or otherwise, without a *tres leches* cake (mine has four, not three milks!) or a flan. The difference with my version is that, like my savory recipes, I'm always looking to add a pinch, a squeeze, or a drizzle of a little something extra special.

Simple recipes, like pears poached in red wine, are just right for when you need to make a dessert in advance—they're so easy that they practically poach themselves. Fresh fruit becomes decadent when paired with a rich white chocolate sauce or caramelized with just enough sugar to enhance their sweetness.

The White Chocolate and Raspberry Bread Pudding, Mango Quatres Leches, and Maruja's Flan are all make-ahead friendly and excellent for potlucks. From indulgent sweets like the sticky rice pudding with dulce de leche to lean ones like the super creamy peach cups, this chapter is all about satisfying the sweet tooth in all of us.

PEARS AL VINO TINTO

3 cups red wine (such as pinot noir)

1 cup sugar

3 whole black peppercorns

3 whole cloves

Three 1/2-inch-wide strips lemon peel

1 cinnamon stick

4 ripe Bartlett or Bosc pears, peeled, halved, and cored

1 pint vanilla ice cream (optional)

1/2 teaspoon freshly grated nutmeg

A red wine–poached pear takes on a velvety texture and ruby-red tint. Spices, like black peppercorns, cloves, and cinnamon, add a mulled taste to the poaching brew, while lemon peel gives it a fresh, citrusy note. The pears become so tender and infused with flavor that you don't even need to top them with ice cream if you're looking for a lighter dessert—but the combo of the warm poached pear, good-quality vanilla ice cream, and sweet poaching syrup is hard to beat. The poached pears can be refrigerated in the poaching liquid for up to two days.

1. Bring the red wine, sugar, peppercorns, cloves, lemon strips, cinnamon stick, and 1/2 cup of water to a boil in a large pot over high heat, stirring occasionally to dissolve the sugar, about 5 minutes. Reduce the heat to medium-low and simmer the mixture until slightly reduced, about 2 minutes.

2. Add the pears and simmer until they're tender and a paring knife easily slips into the center, about 15 minutes. Use a slotted spoon to transfer the pears to a large bowl and set aside.

3. Remove and discard the peppercorns, cloves, lemon peel, and cinnamon stick. Continue to simmer the poaching liquid over medium-low heat until it is reduced by half and is the consistency of a thick syrup, about 30 minutes.

4. Return the pears to the thick poaching liquid and heat for 1 minute, basting the pears with the syrup. Turn off the heat and place 2 pears halves in the center of each plate or bowl. Drizzle the pears with 2 tablespoons each of the poaching syrup, and then top with a scoop of vanilla ice cream, if using, and a pinch of nutmeg.

CARAMELIZED VANILLA FIGS *with*
GOAT CHEESE *and* GRILLED PAPAYAS

Serves 4

1 vanilla bean, halved lengthwise

Juice of 1 large orange

1/2 cup mango juice

1/4 cup agave syrup

1 1/2 teaspoons fresh lemon juice

2 small papayas, halved lengthwise, seeds removed

2 cups fresh black mission figs, stemmed and halved

2 tablespoons crumbled fresh goat cheese

1/4 cup finely chopped fresh mint

Grilling introduces a whole new dimension of flavor to ripe fruit, such as honey-sweet papayas. The figs are poached in mango juice with vanilla and topped with a little goat cheese and chopped mint. The salty tanginess of the cheese totally balances the sweetness of the fruit, making a dessert that pleases on every level.

1. Use the back of a paring knife to scrape the vanilla seeds from the bean and then add the seeds and bean to a medium saucepan. Pour in the orange juice, mango juice, agave syrup, and lemon juice and add 1/2 cup of water. Bring to a boil over high heat until it becomes like maple syrup in consistency, about 10 minutes. Place the papaya halves on a large plate cut side up and brush 1/4 cup of the syrup over them. Set aside.

2. Add the figs to the remaining sauce in the saucepan and cook over low heat, stirring occasionally, until the figs are tender but still hold their shape and the liquid is thick and reduced by half, 10 to 12 minutes. Turn off the heat and use a slotted spoon to transfer the figs to a medium bowl. Set the sauce aside.

3. Prepare a medium-hot charcoal or gas grill.

4. Set the papayas cut side down on the grill, cover, and cook until the papayas have grill marks, 5 to 6 minutes.

5. Use tongs to transfer each papaya half to a plate. Divide the figs among the papayas, then drizzle with the remaining sauce. Sprinkle with the goat cheese and mint and serve.

CAPPUCCINO *and* BISCOTTI CUPS

1 cup sweetened condensed milk

3 tablespoons dark rum

2½ tablespoons instant espresso powder

8 ounces mascarpone cheese

2 teaspoons pure vanilla extract

1½ cups heavy cream

2 tablespoons sugar

½ pound vanilla biscotti (about 4 large cookies)

¼ cup unsweetened cocoa powder or 2 tablespoons instant espresso powder for serving (optional)

Shaved dark chocolate for serving (optional)

This dessert is a Latin spin on the classic Italian dessert tiramisù. Here rum is used instead of coffee liqueur to flavor the cream base, and sweetened condensed milk instead of eggs or gelatin to thicken the mascarpone cheese. Biscotti stands in for ladyfingers, lending a great crunch to the otherwise creamy dessert. The cappuccino cups can be refrigerated for up to one day before serving.

1. Heat ½ cup of the condensed milk and ¾ cup of water in a small saucepan over medium heat, stirring occasionally, until it comes to a boil. Turn off the heat and whisk in the rum and espresso powder, stirring until the espresso powder is dissolved. Set aside.

2. Using an electric mixer, blend the mascarpone cheese, the remaining ½ cup condensed milk, and the vanilla until smooth. In a separate bowl, whip the cream with the sugar until the mixture holds tall, stiff peaks (when the whisk attachment is lifted out of the bowl, the peak should stand straight without drooping).

3. Whisk one-quarter of the whipped cream into the mascarpone mixture to lighten the mascarpone. Whisk in the remaining whipped cream until completely combined.

4. Place the biscotti in a gallon-size resealable plastic bag and, using a rolling pin or the bottom of a heavy skillet, crush the biscotti until the crumbs are rough textured and there are still small, bite-size bits (you don't want fine crumbs). Divide one-third of the biscotti crumbs among four 6-ounce cappuccino cups and then drizzle the crumbs with 1 to 2 tablespoons

of the espresso syrup (enough to flavor the crumbs but not make them soft and mushy). Divide half of the mascarpone mixture among the cups, spreading it in an even layer over the crumbs. Repeat with one-half of the remaining biscotti crumbs and with the remaining espresso syrup and the remaining mascarpone mixture. Divide the remaining biscotti crumbs over each serving. Cover each cup with a sheet of plastic wrap and refrigerate for at least 2 hours or up to 1 day before serving. Dust with the cocoa powder, if using. Finish with shaved chocolate, if using, and serve.

Sabes Qué?

Use a vegetable peeler to shave strips off a chunk of chocolate to create pretty chocolate ribbons or shards.

FRESH BERRIES *and*
GOLDEN CHOCOLATE SAUCE

Serves 6

1 cup milk

2 vanilla beans, halved lengthwise

½ cup sweetened condensed milk

8 ounces white chocolate, finely chopped

1 cup fresh blackberries

1 cup fresh raspberries

1 cup fresh strawberries, hulled

6 small fresh mint sprigs

Fresh in-season berries picked at the peak of ripeness are unbeatable, except when you drizzle a little warm and caramel-y white chocolate sauce over them. The key to a deeply golden sauce is to let the sugars in the white chocolate and sweetened condensed milk cook low and slow until it's just the right shade of pale butterscotch. Any leftover sauce can be refrigerated for up to one week. It's fantastic as a dipping sauce for fresh strawberries or spooned over French toast, waffles, or a scoop of ice cream.

1. Pour the milk into a medium saucepan. Use the back of a paring knife to scrape the vanilla seeds from the bean and then add the seeds and bean to the milk. Cook the mixture over medium-low heat, stirring occasionally, until the vanilla is fragrant, about 10 minutes (if the milk starts to bubble up, reduce the heat).

2. Add the condensed milk and white chocolate and cook, stirring occasionally, until the chocolate is melted and the mixture is thick and the color of butterscotch, about 25 minutes. Turn off the heat and set aside to cool for 5 to 10 minutes.

3. Place the blackberries, raspberries, and strawberries in a large bowl and gently toss them together. Divide the berries among six bowls, drizzle with the white chocolate sauce, and finish with a mint sprig before serving.

SPICY CHOCOLATE MOUSSE

- 4 large egg yolks
- 1 jalapeño pepper, grated on the small holes of a box grater or with a Microplane
- 8 ounces semisweet or bittersweet chocolate (around 67% cacao), finely chopped
- 4 tablespoons (½ stick) unsalted butter
- 2 teaspoons ground cinnamon
- ½ teaspoon cayenne pepper, plus extra for serving (optional)
- 3 tablespoons dark rum
- 2 cups heavy cream
- 1 cup sugar
- 6 large strawberries, hulled

Chocolate mousse with jalapeños? You bet! The sharpness of green chiles adds an unexpected bite to the chocolate mousse, while a little cayenne pepper gives a slow burn to the finish. The spiciness is countered by sugar, good quality chocolate (I like using chocolate that has at least 67% cocoa solids), and the natural, sweet richness of heavy cream. Spicy chocolate mousse is the perfect ending to a rich meal.

1. Fill a medium saucepan with 2 inches of water and bring it to a boil. Lower the heat to medium-low. Whisk the egg yolks in a large heatproof bowl and then whisk in ¼ cup of water and the jalapeño. Place the bowl with the eggs over the saucepan of hot water and whisk constantly until the volume doubles and the eggs are thick like soft whipped cream, about 2 minutes. Remove the bowl from the saucepan (keep the heat on under the pan) and set aside.

2. Place the chopped chocolate, butter, cinnamon, and cayenne in another large heatproof bowl and place it over the hot water. Let the mixture sit over the water for a few minutes until the butter begins to melt, and then stir the mixture occasionally until the chocolate is completely melted and the mixture is combined. Remove the bowl from the saucepan and set aside.

3. Place a fine-mesh sieve over the bowl with the chocolate mixture. Use a rubber spatula to transfer the egg mixture from its bowl to the sieve. Push the egg mixture through the sieve using the spatula. Once the eggs are strained, whisk in the rum. Continue to whisk the mixture to cool it off, about 4 minutes.

continued

4. Using an electric mixer, whip the cream with the sugar until the mixture holds medium-soft peaks. Scrape one-quarter of the whipped cream into the bowl with the chocolate mixture and gently fold it in to combine. Add one-third of the remaining whipped cream, folding it in gently. Cover the remaining whipped cream with plastic wrap and refrigerate until ready to serve.

5. Divide the chocolate mousse among six 4-ounce glasses or ramekins. Using the back of a spoon, smooth out the top, and then cover each serving with plastic wrap. Refrigerate the mousse for at least 2 hours or up to 8 hours. Before serving, place a dollop of the reserved whipped cream over each cup of mousse and place a strawberry on top, along with a pinch of cayenne, if using.

CREAMY PEACH CUPS
with BRÛLÉED PEACHES

9 ripe peaches

3/4 cup agave syrup

1 envelope unflavored gelatin (about 1 tablespoon)

1 vanilla bean, halved lengthwise, seeds scraped away and reserved, or 1 teaspoon pure vanilla extract

2 tablespoons fresh lemon juice

1 cup reduced-fat cream cheese

Whipped Cream (page 213) for serving (optional)

6 fresh mint sprigs for serving

I developed this dessert for a guest appearance on the NBC show *The Biggest Loser*. You'd never guess from its supercreamy, almost ice cream–like texture that it has only 140 calories per serving. It's the kind of dessert that feels indulgent and sinful but is actually very bikini friendly. The peach cups can be refrigerated for up to one day before serving. If peaches aren't in season, use mangoes, papayas, or fresh berries instead.

1. Place 6 of the peaches on a cutting board. Using a serrated vegetable peeler or a sharp paring knife, peel, halve, and pit the peaches, and then chop them into 1-inch pieces. Place the chopped peaches, 1/2 cup of the agave syrup, and 1 cup of water in a small saucepan and bring to a simmer over medium-low heat. Cook, stirring occasionally, until the peaches are soft, about 5 minutes. Turn off the heat and set aside.

2. Pour 2 tablespoons of warm water into a small bowl. Sprinkle the gelatin over the water, stir, and set aside for 5 minutes to soften.

3. Transfer the peaches and all but 2 tablespoons of the peach juices to a blender jar (set aside the 2 tablespoons peach juices for serving). Add the vanilla bean seeds or the vanilla extract and the gelatin mixture to the blender and process for 1 minute to combine. Add the lemon juice and cream cheese and blend on high speed until the mixture is silky and smooth, and the texture of the puree is airy and thick, like a mousse, 6 to 8 minutes.

4. Divide the puree among six 4-ounce ramekins and cover each ramekin flush with plastic wrap. Refrigerate until the mixture is set, at least 2 1/2 hours or up to 24 hours.

continued

5. Before serving, prepare a medium-low charcoal or gas grill.

6. Halve and pit the remaining 3 peaches and place them on a large plate. Drizzle the peaches with the remaining $1/4$ cup agave syrup and then grill them cut side down until they have grill marks, about 2 minutes.

7. Remove the ramekins from the refrigerator and top with a dollop of whipped cream, if using. Serve each peach cup on a small plate with a grilled peach on the side. Drizzle the reserved peach juice over the cups. Finish with a mint sprig and serve.

Sabes Qué?

Vanilla beans are expensive so you should get as much out of them as you can. After scraping the seeds from the pod (use a paring knife to slice the pod from tip to tip, open the bean, and use the blunt side of the knife to scrape out the seeds), save the pod and add it to a jar of granulated sugar to infuse it with flavor. You can also drop the pod into a bottle of vodka or rum, or let the pod dry out and then grind it with sugar in a spice grinder to make vanilla sugar.

STICKY ARROZ *con* DULCE DE LECHE

Serves 6

6 cups milk

1 cup long-grain white rice (such as basmati)

2 cinnamon sticks

1 whole star anise

One 14-ounce can dulce de leche–style condensed milk

When I was growing up, my mom made this traditional Latin rice pudding dessert for me all the time. This version is made with dulce de leche, which is milk slowly reduced with sugar until it turns caramel-y and brown. You can use the store-bought prepared kind as a shortcut and still find the flavor totally delicious. The smell alone will drive you crazy. While the pudding can be served warm, at room temperature, or chilled, it is best eaten the same day that it is made.

1. Bring the milk, rice, cinnamon sticks, and star anise to a boil in a large heavy-bottomed pot over high heat. Reduce the heat to medium-low and cook, stirring often, until the rice is tender, about 30 minutes. (If the rice starts to stick to the bottom of the pot, reduce the heat to low so it doesn't burn.) Remove and discard the cinnamon sticks and star anise.

2. Pour in the dulce de leche and cook, stirring often, until thickened, about 20 minutes. Divide the rice pudding among six bowls and serve.

MARUJA'S FLAN

Serves 6

1 cup sugar

8 large eggs

1 teaspoon pure vanilla extract

2 12-ounce cans sweetened condensed milk

2 12-ounce cans evaporated milk

This recipe comes from Maruja, my dear friend Juanqui's mother, and I cooked it by her side, diligently taking notes all the while. I must say that it's the best, creamiest, and silkiest flan I have ever had. There is nothing special in the few ingredients—the trick is in how you make it. Number one: Don't overbeat the egg mixture. Number two: Use newspaper to create a cushioned bain marie (water bath). Number three: Bake the flan at 340°F and don't be tempted to go to 350°F. I've done it, and the flan is not the same. The cooked flan can be refrigerated for up to two days and served chilled.

1. Preheat the oven to 340°F. Line a roasting pan with two sheets of newspaper and set aside.

2. Place the sugar in a small heavy-bottomed saucepan over medium heat. Once the sugar begins to melt, stir it every 30 seconds until it is light amber in color, about 8 minutes. Reduce the heat to low and continue to cook the sugar, swirling the pan often, until it is a deep reddish brown, 5 to 7 minutes longer. Immediately remove the pan from the heat and pour the hot sugar (be very careful) into a 9-inch round cake pan. Tilt the pan to cover its entire bottom and up three-quarters of the side with the hot sugar. Set the pan aside.

3. Using an electric mixer, beat the eggs until just combined, about 20 seconds. Add the vanilla, condensed milk, and evaporated milk and beat on medium speed until the mixture is aerated and well combined, about 30 seconds (don't overbeat the mixture—it is very important to beat just until it is combined). Pour the mixture into the sugar-coated pie plate.

4. Carefully place the pan in the newspaper-lined roasting pan. Pour in enough warm water to fill the roasting pan to a depth of 1 inch. Set the roasting pan in the oven and bake the flan until a cake tester inserted into the center of the flan comes out clean, about 1 hour and 15 minutes. Carefully remove the roasting pan from the oven and let cool for 2 hours. After two hours, chill the flan in the refrigerator for at least 2 hours and up to overnight.

5. Remove the flan from the pie plate. Run a paring knife around the edges of the flan. Invert a large serving platter (larger than the flan) over the top of the flan and carefully flip it over so the flan and caramel are released onto the plate. Slice into wedges and serve.

Sabes Qué?

The best way to clean the hot or hardened caramel out of the pan is to cover it with an inch or two of water and bring the water to a boil. The hard sugar will dissolve into the boiling water, making cleanup very quick and simple.

WHITE CHOCOLATE *and* RASPBERRY BREAD PUDDING

Serves 8

1 tablespoon unsalted butter, softened

4 plain day-old croissants, cut into 1-inch cubes

3 cups heavy cream

1 vanilla bean, halved lengthwise

4 ounces white chocolate, finely chopped

1/4 cup dark rum

2 tablespoons sugar

1 pint fresh raspberries

4 large eggs

2 large egg yolks

Whipped Cream (page 213) for serving (optional)

Torta de pan is Venezuela's version of bread pudding, made with condensed milk for extra creaminess and spiked with rum for a kick. I make mine with flaky croissants, and instead of condensed milk, I make a silky white chocolate sauce that gets poured over croissant cubes and fresh raspberries. It bakes into a rich custard, creating an incredibly elegant yet simple dessert—especially when they're baked in individual portions.

1. Preheat the oven to 350°F. Grease a 9-inch square baking dish with the butter.

2. Spread the croissant cubes out in an even layer in the bottom of the prepared baking dish. Set aside.

3. Pour the cream into a medium saucepan. Use the back of a paring knife to scrape the vanilla seeds from the bean and add both to the cream. Stir in the white chocolate. Heat over medium-low heat, stirring often, until the white chocolate is melted, about 5 minutes. Turn off the heat and set aside.

4. In a small saucepan, heat the rum, sugar, and 1/4 cup of water over medium-low heat, stirring often, until the sugar is dissolved, about 10 minutes. Place the raspberries in a medium bowl and pour the rum syrup over the berries. Gently stir to combine. Cover the croissant cubes with the rum-soaked raspberries and syrup.

5. Whisk together the eggs and egg yolks in a large bowl. Remove the vanilla bean from the white chocolate mixture and then whisk about 1 cup of the white chocolate mixture into the eggs. Once the bottom of the bowl is warm (you may need to add 1/2 to 1 cup more of the white chocolate mixture to sufficiently temper the eggs so they don't curdle), whisk in

continued

the remaining white chocolate mixture. Use a rubber spatula to scrape this mixture evenly over the raspberries and croissant cubes.

6. Place the pan with the bread pudding in a roasting pan. Fill the roasting pan with enough warm water to reach halfway up the sides of the baking dish. Bake for about 20 minutes, or until the center of the pudding is set and a cake tester inserted into the center comes out clean. Remove from the oven and cool completely. Serve with a dollop of whipped cream, if using.

MANGO QUATRO LECHES

Serves 10

Nonstick vegetable cooking spray

2 cups all-purpose flour

3/4 cup plus 1/2 teaspoon sugar

2 teaspoons baking soda

1/2 teaspoon kosher salt

4 large eggs, separated

1 teaspoon pure vanilla extract

2 large egg whites

3/4 cup unsweetened coconut flakes

1 cup chopped mangoes

2 cups fat-free half-and-half

One 14-ounce can fat-free sweetened condensed milk

One 12-ounce can low-fat 2% evaporated milk

2 tablespoons fresh orange juice

1/2 cup store-bought dulce de leche

1 cup Whipped Cream (page 213)

Tres leches cake is very big in Latin America. Made with whole milk, sweetened condensed milk, and evaporated milk, it is a dense and moist cake that is sweet and simple, too, great for casual parties and birthdays. I wanted to create an even more indulgent approach, with mangoes serving as a fruity bottom layer to the cake and dulce de leche (the fourth milk) drizzled over the top.

1. Preheat the oven to 350°F. Coat a 9 by 13-inch springform pan with nonstick vegetable cooking spray and set aside.

2. Whisk together the flour, 3/4 cup of the sugar, the baking soda, and the salt in a large bowl.

3. Using an electric mixer, beat the egg yolks, vanilla, and 1/4 teaspoon of the sugar on medium-high speed until the yolks are pale yellow and doubled in volume. In another large bowl, beat the 6 egg whites with the remaining 1/4 teaspoon sugar on medium-high speed until they form soft peaks. Whisk one-quarter of the egg whites into the egg yolk mixture and then gently fold in the remaining whites until just a few white streaks remain. Sift in the flour mixture and gently fold it into the egg mixture.

4. Use a rubber spatula to scrape the mixture into the prepared springform pan. Bake for 35 to 45 minutes, or until a cake tester inserted into the center comes out clean. Remove from the oven but do not turn off the heat. Set the cake aside on a wire rack to cool completely before running a paring knife around the edge of the cake to loosen it and then turning it out onto a flat plate or cooling rack. Clean the pan and set it aside.

continued

5. While the cake cools, spread the coconut onto a rimmed baking sheet and toast it in the oven, stirring occasionally, until it's fragrant and golden brown, 5 to 8 minutes. Remove from the oven and turn the coconut out onto a large plate to cool.

6. Spread the mangoes out in an even layer in the bottom of the clean cake pan. Place the cooled cake on top of the mangoes. Whisk the half-and-half, condensed milk, evaporated milk, and orange juice in a large bowl. Pour the mixture over the cake. Cover the pan with plastic wrap and refrigerate for at least 30 minutes or up to 2 days to allow the cake to absorb the liquid.

7. Remove the cake from the refrigerator. Slice the cake into pieces and serve with a drizzle of the dulce de leche and some whipped cream. Sprinkle the toasted coconut over the top.

HONEY *and* MARSALA-SPIKED PEACHES *and* STRAWBERRIES *with* SABAYON

Serves 8

FOR THE FRUIT

- 3/4 cup sweet Marsala wine
- 3/4 cup sugar
- 3 tablespoons honey
- 2 tablespoons bottled balsamic glaze
- 4 ripe peaches, peeled, pitted, and diced into 1/2-inch pieces
- 1 quart strawberries, hulled and diced into 1/2-inch pieces

FOR THE SABAYON

- 8 large egg yolks
- 1/4 cup sugar
- 1/4 cup sweet Marsala wine
- 2 cups heavy cream

Fresh fruit for dessert gets extra special treatment when soaked in honey and sherrylike Marsala wine and then topped with this lusciously rich dessert sauce that has a texture somewhere between crème anglaise and custard. Called zabaglione in Italian and sabayon in Spanish and French, I give my version a special edge by adding a few tablespoons of tangy-sweet and syrupy bottled balsamic glaze to the honey marinade for the fruit.

1. Place the 3/4 cup Marsala wine, sugar, honey, and balsamic glaze in a small saucepan and bring to a simmer over medium heat, stirring occasionally, until the sugar is dissolved. Place the peaches and strawberries in a large bowl, pour the hot syrup over the fruit, and set aside.

2. Fill a large pot with 2 inches of water and bring it to a simmer over high heat. Reduce the heat to low. Whisk the egg yolks, sugar, and 1/4 cup of Marsala wine together in a large heat-safe bowl and place the bowl over the pot with the hot water (the bottom of the bowl shouldn't touch the water otherwise the eggs will scramble). Constantly whisk the egg mixture over the hot water until it becomes fluffy and thick, about 10 minutes. Turn off the heat of the water bath, remove the bowl, and continue to vigorously whisk the egg mixture until it has doubled in volume and has cooled, 2 to 3 minutes.

3. Pour the cream into the bowl of a stand mixer and whip it on medium-high speed to medium-stiff peaks. Fold the whipped cream into the Marsala sauce.

4. Divide the fruit between 8 martini glasses or dessert cups. Top with the sabayon and serve.

THE BASICS

Modern Latin cooking is a mix of cultures and cuisines in which Latin ingredients add an edge to the flavors and foods we know and love. It's a way of honoring the traditions of home while embracing new dishes from around the world that we as Americans have come to love.

There are several ingredients and recipes that I count on to bring that extra layer of flavor to my food. Some are Latin and some aren't. Some, like sofrito, red wine demi-glaze, and chicken stock, build flavor from within, while others, like salsitas and herb drizzles, finish a dish with a punch of flavor. In this section, you'll find recipes that I consider essential to the New Latin kitchen.

SPICY GUASACACA SALSITA

Makes 2 cups

1 Hass avocado, halved, pitted, and peeled

1/2 cup finely chopped fresh cilantro

2 tablespoons fresh lime juice

2 teaspoons kosher salt

1 1/2 teaspoons Tabasco sauce

This Venezuelan-style guacamole-like sauce has a pungent top note thanks to piquant Tabasco sauce. It sometimes gets pureed and served as a sauce as in the Chilled Shrimp and Peruvian Corn Salad (page 70).

Place the avocado halves in the bowl of a food processor and blend until completely smooth. Scrape the mixture into a medium bowl and stir in the cilantro, lime juice, salt, and Tabasco. Transfer to an airtight container and refrigerate for up to 1 day. (Note: The top layer of avocado, which is exposed to air, will start to brown; stir or scrape it away before serving.)

JICAMA-APPLE SALSITA

Makes 3½ cups

1 jicama, peeled and cut into ½-inch cubes

1 green apple, peeled, cored, and cut into ½-inch cubes

1 small red onion, finely chopped

½ cup finely chopped cilantro

¼ cup finely chopped fresh flat-leaf parsley

½ cup extra-virgin olive oil

Juice of 1 lime

1 teaspoon kosher salt

½ teaspoon freshly ground black pepper

Jicama is a juicy root vegetable that is crunchy like an underripe pear, with a flavor reminiscent of apples.

Place the jicama, apples, onions, cilantro, parsley, olive oil, lime juice, salt, and pepper in a medium bowl and stir to combine. Transfer to an airtight container and refrigerate for up to 2 days.

CILANTRO and ROASTED JALAPEÑO SALSA PICANTE

Makes 3½ cups

1 jalapeño pepper

1¼ cups fat-free plain yogurt

1 small yellow onion, roughly chopped

½ Hass avocado, pitted and peeled

½ cup fresh cilantro leaves

½ garlic clove

2 tablespoons extra-virgin olive oil

½ teaspoon fresh lemon juice

½ teaspoon kosher salt

¼ teaspoon ground cumin

This smooth salsa can be drizzled over grilled steak, chicken, pork, or even added to a vinaigrette to give fish a smoky touch.

1. Adjust an oven rack to the upper-middle position and pre-heat the broiler to high.

2. Place the jalapeño in a small baking dish and broil until the chile is charred and deflated, about 10 minutes (check the broiler often as broiler intensity varies), turning the chile midway through cooking. Remove the baking dish from the oven and set the chile aside to cool for 10 minutes. Peel off the charred skin, halve the chile, and scrape away the seeds.

3. Place the jalapeño, yogurt, onions, avocado, cilantro, garlic, olive oil, lemon juice, salt, and cumin in the bowl of a food processor. Add 2 tablespoons of water and blend until smooth. Transfer to an airtight container and refrigerate for up to 3 days.

ROASTED HABANERO SALSITA

Makes 3¹/₂ cups

1 large red bell pepper

1 plum tomato

1 habanero chile

1 garlic clove, unpeeled

1¹/₄ cups fat-free plain yogurt

1 small yellow onion, roughly chopped

¹/₂ Hass avocado, peeled

2 tablespoons extra-virgin olive oil

¹/₂ teaspoon fresh lemon juice

¹/₂ teaspoon kosher salt

¹/₄ teaspoon ground cumin

A roasted tomato, red bell pepper, and garlic clove curb the habanero's superspicy flavor in this smooth sauce.

1. Preheat the oven to 450°F. Line a rimmed baking sheet with aluminum foil.

2. Place the bell pepper, tomato, habanero, and garlic on the prepared baking sheet. Roast them in the oven until the pepper is soft and the tomato is slightly wrinkled, about 30 minutes, turning the vegetables midway through roasting. Remove the baking sheet from the oven and set aside until they're cool enough to handle, about 10 minutes.

3. Skin the bell pepper, tomato, and chile. Halve and seed them and place them in the bowl of a food processor. Peel the garlic and add it to the food processor, along with the yogurt, onions, avocado, olive oil, lemon juice, salt, cumin, and 2 tablespoons of water. Blend until smooth. Transfer to an airtight container and refrigerate for up to 3 days.

INFUSED OILS

Oils infused with different flavoring agents add depth to food, and come in especially handy when you're cooking a meal quickly. Oil infusions are simple to make, and once you have one or two around, you'll find yourself reaching for them again and again. Just about anything can be infused into oil, from garlic to dried chiles and even citrus, so be open to letting your imagination lead you to new taste discoveries. Infused oils should be refrigerated and will stay fresh for about 1 week. Oil solidifies in the refrigerator, so let it sit out on a counter for 20 minutes before using (if you're using your oven, place it on top of your stove to liquefy quickly). Or place the bottle with oil in it in a large bowl or pitcher of warm water to heat it gently before using. Use oil infusions to:

* Drizzle over grilled fish, chicken, or steak.
* Toss with vegetables before roasting.
* Sprinkle into a bowl of soup.
* Whisk into a vinaigrette.
* Sauté with vegetables.
* Pour into a small bowl as a dipping sauce for fresh bread.
* Puree with fresh herbs, Parmigiano-Reggiano cheese, and pine nuts for pesto.

The following are a few infused oils that I like to keep on hand, but feel free to experiment with ingredients and discover your own favorites.

SPICY CHERRY PEPPER OIL

Makes about 2 cups

1 cup extra-virgin olive oil
1 cup jarred pickled cherry peppers

1. Pour the olive oil into a small saucepan and heat over medium-low heat until the oil is warmed through.

2. Place the peppers in the bowl of a food processor and puree. With the machine running, slowly pour the warm olive oil into the food processor. Stop the machine once the mixture is smooth. Transfer to an airtight container or jar and set aside for at least 1 hour before using.

INFUSED TOMATO OIL

Makes about 2 cups

1 **cup extra-virgin olive oil**
1 **large tomato, halved and seeded**

1. Pour the olive oil into a small saucepan and heat over medium-low heat until the oil is warmed through.

2. Place the tomato in the bowl of a food processor and puree. With the machine running, slowly pour the warm olive oil into the food processor. Stop the machine once the mixture is smooth. Transfer to an airtight container or jar and set aside for at least 1 hour before using.

INFUSED CILANTRO OIL

Makes about 1¹/₂ cups

¹/₂ **cup cilantro leaves**
1¹/₂ **cups extra-virgin olive oil**

1. Place the cilantro in a quart-size resealable plastic freezer bag, removing as much air as possible from the bag before sealing. Lay the bag flat and shake slightly so the leaves are in somewhat of a single layer. Place the bag flat in the freezer overnight (or for up to 2 weeks) to allow the leaves to fully freeze before using. NOTE: Basil can be used in place of cilantro.

2. Pour the olive oil into a small saucepan and heat over medium-low heat until the oil is warmed through.

3. Place the frozen cilantro in the bowl of a food processor and process until finely chopped. With the machine running, slowly pour the warm olive oil into the food processor. Stop the machine once the mixture is smooth. Transfer to an airtight container or jar and set aside for at least 1 hour before using.

HERB DRIZZLE

Makes about 1/3 cup

1 tablespoon finely chopped fresh cilantro

1 tablespoon finely chopped fresh flat-leaf parsley

1/2 teaspoon finely chopped fresh thyme

1/4 cup extra-virgin olive oil

Pinch of kosher salt

Pinch of freshly ground black pepper

Introduce a wonderful herby flavor to everything from vinaigrettes to grilled fish, soups, and roasted vegetables.

Stir together the cilantro, parsley, and thyme in a small bowl. Add the olive oil, salt, and pepper and whisk to combine. Transfer to an airtight container and refrigerate for up to 3 days. Let the drizzle sit out at room temperature before using.

CANDIED RED PEPPERS

Makes 1/2 cup

1 cup sugar

1 cup distilled white vinegar

2 large red bell peppers, halved, seeded, and sliced lengthwise into 1/4-inch-wide strips

1 garlic clove, smashed

1 cinnamon stick

1 star anise

Simmering bell peppers in sugar and vinegar transforms them into a jewel-like sweet-tart condiment that adds a wonderful piquant taste to Churrasco Steak and Arugula with Candied Pepper Chimichurri (page 123).

Dissolve the sugar in the vinegar in a medium pot over medium heat, stirring occasionally. Add the bell peppers, garlic, cinnamon stick, and star anise and reduce the heat to low. Cook until the bell pepper strips are glazed, candied, and somewhat transparent, about 45 minutes. Turn off the heat and set aside to cool. Transfer the bell peppers and liquid to an airtight container and refrigerate for up to 1 month.

BASIC SOFRITO

Makes 2¹/₂ cups

2 tablespoons extra-virgin olive oil

2 yellow onions, finely chopped

2 garlic cloves, very finely minced

4 fresh ají dulce chiles (about ¹/₂ cup), halved and finely chopped

2 scallions, white and light green parts only, finely chopped

1 celery stalk (with leaves), finely chopped

1 leek, white and light green parts only, finely chopped

1 red bell pepper, halved, seeded and finely chopped

2 tomatoes, halved, seeded, and finely chopped

Sofrito is the base of many Latin dishes. Just as the French use mirepoix, a combination of finely chopped onions, carrots, and celery, Latin Americans use a sofrito to build flavor in soups, stews, and sauces. If you can't find ají dulce, use seeded jalapeños or jarred pickled cherry peppers.

Heat the olive oil in a large skillet over high heat. Add the onions and garlic and cook until the onions are translucent, stirring often, for about 2 minutes. Stir in the ají dulce, scallions, celery, leeks, and bell peppers and cook, stirring occasionally, until the bell peppers are tender, about 5 minutes. Add the tomatoes and cook, stirring, until the juices evaporate, 2 to 3 minutes. Use immediately, or cool to room temperature before scraping into an airtight container and refrigerating for up to 4 days or freezing for up to 3 months.

HERB TORTILLAS

½ cup masa harina

½ teaspoon kosher salt

2 tablespoons finely chopped fresh cilantro

2 tablespoons finely chopped fresh mint

2 tablespoons finely chopped fresh flat-leaf parsley

Homemade tortillas are addictively delicious and simple to make. Fresh cilantro, mint, and parsley make them all the more tasty. Omit the herbs for a plain corn tortilla.

1. Whisk together the masa harina, salt, cilantro, mint, and parsley in a medium bowl. Add ⅔ cup of warm water and use a wooden spoon to mix together. Once the dough becomes too hard to mix with a spoon, use your hands to knead it until it comes together in a smooth consistency, about 5 minutes.

2. Turn out the dough onto a cutting board and divide it into 8 pieces. Roll each piece into a ball and place the balls on a large plate. Cover the plate with a damp kitchen towel so the dough doesn't dry out.

3. Heat a large nonstick skillet or a flattop griddle over high heat. Line the bottom and top plates of a tortilla press with plastic wrap. Place a ball of dough on the bottom plate and press to make an almost paper-thin 3-inch tortilla. Open the press and use the plastic wrap to lift the tortilla off the press. Peel the top layer of plastic wrap off the tortilla and invert the tortilla onto the hot skillet (it should sizzle). Cook until toasted, about 1 minute, and then use your fingers or a spatula to flip over the tortilla and cook the other side until golden and crispy, about 1 minute longer. Transfer to a tortilla warmer or serve immediately. Repeat with the remaining balls of dough.

BASIC WHITE RICE

Serves 4

- 2 cups long-grain white rice (preferably jasmine)
- 1 tablespoon unsalted butter
- 1½ teaspoons extra-virgin olive oil
- 1 teaspoon kosher salt
- 4 cups Chicken Stock (page 211) or store-bought chicken broth

This is the way both my grandmother and mother make their buttery, fluffy white rice. The secret to its amazing texture is to keep the pan covered for the last 20 minutes of cooking—no peeking!

1. Place the rice, butter, olive oil, salt, and chicken stock in a large saucepan. Bring the liquid to a boil over high heat and cook, uncovered, until there are holes on the surface of the rice that tunnel down to the bottom of the pot, about 15 minutes.

2. Reduce the heat to the lowest setting, cover the pan, and continue cooking for 20 minutes. Uncover the pan, fluff the rice with a fork, and serve.

BEST BLACK BEANS

Serves 6

½ pound dried black beans (about 1¼ cups)

1 bay leaf

2 tablespoons extra-virgin olive oil

1 yellow onion, finely chopped

1 large green bell pepper, halved, seeded, and finely chopped

10 garlic cloves, very finely minced

2 teaspoons ground cumin

2 teaspoons dried oregano

1 teaspoon ground coriander

1 tablespoon red wine vinegar, plus extra for serving

1 tablespoon kosher salt

Pinch of cayenne pepper

Freshly ground black pepper

Black beans are a staple at the Latin table, where they're spooned over rice at nearly every meal. Using dried beans instead of canned contributes a wonderful richness to the bean broth and also cooks up with a creamier consistency than canned beans. If your prefer the speed of canned beans, substitute two 15-ounce cans of rinsed black beans for the dried beans.

1. Place the beans in a large soup pot with 12 cups of water and the bay leaf and bring to a boil over high heat. Cover, turn off the heat, and set aside for 1 hour.

2. Return the beans to a simmer over high heat. Uncover the pot, reduce the heat to medium-low, and simmer until soft, about 1½ hours.

3. Heat the olive oil in a medium skillet over medium-high heat. Add the onions and bell peppers and cook, stirring often, until they're soft, about 5 minutes. Stir in the garlic, cumin, oregano, and coriander, cooking until the garlic is fragrant, about 1 minute. Turn off the heat and scrape the onion mixture into the beans. Continue cooking the beans until they're very tender and the liquid is slightly thick, about 1½ hours longer (if the liquid seems too thick after 1½ hours, adjust the consistency by adding some water).

4. Stir in the vinegar, salt, cayenne, and black pepper to taste and serve with more vinegar on the side.

SWEET PLANTAINS MADUROS

Serves 4

Nonstick vegetable cooking spray
4 ripe, black plantains
Kosher salt
1 lime, cut into wedges

Plantains look like large bananas. They are sold in various stages of ripeness—when the skins are green, they are starchy like a potato and often sliced and fried to make *tostones*. When the skins turn black, they are sticky sweet inside, perfect for making maduros. Usually sweet maduros are fried and served with *crema* (more like créme fraîche than sour cream), but I prefer to oven bake them and finish them with salt and lime for a sweet-salty-citrusy side.

1. Preheat the oven to 350°F. Line a rimmed baking sheet with aluminum foil, lightly coat the foil with nonstick vegetable cooking spray, and set aside.

2. Peel the plantains and cut them in half crosswise on a diagonal, then cut each half in half lengthwise. Place the plantains on the prepared baking sheet and bake for about 20 minutes, until fragrant, golden brown, and crisp around the edges. Remove from the oven and set aside to cool.

3. Transfer the plantains to a paper towel–lined plate and sprinkle with salt. Serve hot with lime wedges.

TOMATO SAUCE

Makes 3½ cups

One 14-ounce can crushed tomatoes

One 8-ounce bottle tomato sauce, strained

1 carrot, roughly chopped

1 red onion, roughly chopped

1 celery stalk, roughly chopped

1 tablespoon sugar

1 teaspoon kosher salt

½ teaspoon freshly ground black pepper

I use tomato sauce as a base for pasta and even as a broth (Tomato Broth with Clams and Crisp Calamari, page 10). It's basic, delicious, and endlessly versatile.

Place the crushed tomatoes, tomato sauce, carrots, onions, celery, sugar, salt, and pepper in a blender jar and puree until completely smooth. Transfer to an airtight container and re-frigerate for up to 3 days or freeze in a quart-size resealable plastic freezer bag for up to 2 weeks.

SIMPLIFIED RED WINE DEMI-GLAZE

Makes 5 cups

1½ pounds beef, chicken, pork, or
    veal bones

4 carrots, cut into thirds

4 celery stalks, cut into thirds

2 yellow onions, quartered

8 garlic cloves

1 tablespoon extra-virgin olive oil

½ teaspoon kosher salt

    One 6-ounce can tomato paste

1 bottle (750 milliliters) dry red wine
    (such as cabernet sauvignon or
    merlot)

A typical demi-glaze takes days to make. This version condenses the process into a few hours without sacrificing flavor or intensity. The demi-glaze gives structure to sauces like the passion fruit sauce for the Blue Cheese–Crusted Beef Tenderloin with Passion Fruit Demi-Glaze (page 91) and the barbecue sauce for the Mango BBQ Baby Back Ribs (page 119). Try adding it to a pan after searing a chicken breast, pork chop, or skirt steak to make a rich pan sauce.

1. Preheat the oven to 400°F.

2. Place the bones, carrots, celery, onions, and garlic in a large roasting pan. Add the olive oil and salt, toss with the bones and vegetables, and cook for 30 minutes.

3. Whisk the tomato paste in a small bowl to loosen it up. Remove the roasting pan from the oven and use a pastry or silicone brush to coat the bones and vegetables with the tomato paste. Return the pan to the oven for 30 minutes longer. Turn the bones and any large pieces of vegetables over, and cook for another 20 minutes.

4. Remove the roasting pan from the oven and pour the red wine over the bones and vegetables. Set aside for 5 minutes. Remove the bones from the pan and discard. Use a wooden spoon to scrape up any browned bits from the bottom of the pan and then use a slotted spoon to transfer the vegetables to a large stockpot or soup pot. Pour in the liquid from the roasting pan.

5. Add 6 cups of water to the stockpot and bring to a boil over high heat. Turn down the heat to medium-high and cook

for 10 minutes, then turn down the heat to medium-low and simmer until the liquid is reduced by half, 45 minutes to 1 hour. Turn off the heat and set aside to cool slightly, about 5 minutes.

6. Set a fine-mesh sieve over a large plastic container and strain the reduced demi-glaze into it. Use a rubber spatula to press down on the solids in the sieve to extract as much liquid as possible. Cover the container and refrigerate for up to 3 days or freeze for up to 3 weeks.

BEEF STOCK

Makes 3¹/₂ quarts

2 **pounds beef shanks**

1 **large yellow onion, roughly chopped**

2 **carrots, roughly chopped**

2 **celery stalks, roughly chopped**

1 **large bunch fresh cilantro, with stems**

1 **large bunch fresh mint, with stems**

1. Place 1 gallon of water, the beef shanks, onions, carrots, celery, cilantro, and mint in a large soup pot over high heat and bring to a boil. Cook for 10 minutes, reduce the heat to medium-low, and simmer for 1 hour, skimming the foam off the top of the stock whenever necessary.

2. Turn off the heat and let cool for 30 minutes. Strain the stock through a fine-mesh sieve into a large bowl and discard the solids. Let the stock cool to room temperature. Divide it between two gallon-size resealable plastic bags and refrigerate for up to 3 days, or freeze for up to 3 months.

CHICKEN STOCK

Makes 3½ quarts

1 **pound chicken thighs with skins**
1 **pound chicken wings with skins**
1 **yellow onion, roughly chopped**
2 **carrots, roughly chopped**
2 **celery stalks, roughly chopped**
1 **large bunch fresh cilantro, with stems**
1 **large bunch fresh mint, with stems**

1. Place 1 gallon of water, the chicken thighs, chicken wings, onions, carrots, celery, cilantro, and mint in a large soup pot over high heat and bring to a boil. Cook for 10 minutes, reduce the heat to medium-low, and simmer for 1 hour, skimming the foam off the top of the stock whenever necessary.

2. Turn off the heat and let cool for 30 minutes. Strain the stock through a fine-mesh sieve into a large bowl and discard the solids. Let the stock cool to room temperature. Divide it between two gallon-size resealable plastic bags and refrigerate for up to 3 days, or freeze for up to 3 months.

CARAMELIZED WALNUTS

Makes 2 cups

2 cups raw shelled walnut halves

²/₃ cup sugar

¹/₃ cup Chicken Stock (page 211) or store-bought chicken broth

1. Line a rimmed baking sheet with parchment paper and set aside.

2. Heat a large skillet over medium-high heat. Add the walnuts and sugar and cook, stirring constantly, until the sugar is melted and amber colored, 3 to 4 minutes. Pour in the chicken stock, reduce the heat to medium, and simmer until the stock has evaporated, about 5 minutes.

3. Transfer the walnuts to the prepared baking sheet, spread them out in an even layer, and set aside to cool. Once the nuts have cooled, transfer to an airtight container and store at room temperature for up to 1 week.

WHIPPED CREAM

Makes 2 cups

1 **cup heavy cream**

1 **teaspoon pure vanilla extract**

3 **tablespoons sugar**

Using an electric mixer, whip the cream and vanilla on medium speed until it is thick and frothy. With the mixer running, sprinkle in the sugar and continue to beat until medium-stiff peaks form, about 2 minutes. Use immediately, or cover the mixing bowl with plastic wrap and refrigerate the whipped cream for up to 4 hours. Whisk before using.

ACKNOWLEDGMENTS

I always say that I have the best job in the world because I do what I am passionate about, what I absolutely love, and that is to cook, talk, teach, and live food 24/7. I couldn't do what I do without the help and support of the people around me. First and foremost, I thank God for giving me so many blessings throughout my life. To my mother, Blanca, to whom I owe everything, thank you for giving me the foundation of love and values that is the glue that holds everything else in place. To my stepfather, Jaime, my brother and sister-in-law, Carlos and Lisbeth, my nieces and nephews Andrea, Carlos-Alejandro, Laura, and Caco, thank you for being by my side and understanding that there is such a thing as unconditional love.

To my absolutely wonderful team: Randy Jackson, my manager, who is a wonderful blessing and has opened so many doors to an amazing life; Harriet Sternberg, who is the conductor of Randy's vision; and Natalie Perez, who keeps me organized and shares my goals. Thank you to my agents at William Morris Endeavor Entertainment: Sean Perry, Eric Rovner, Amir Shahkhalili, Miles Gidaly, Andy McNicol, and everyone who works so tirelessly to help me reach out to an ever-widening audience. And a big thanks to my staff, Sarah Daly and Ramiro Arango, as well as my interns Samantha Wong, Natalia Santos, and Alia Asher, who worked so intensely on this book and helped make it a reality.

To my dear friend Soledad O'Brien, thank you for giving me the opportunity to share with the world what I do, and for your sage advice, which I still practice to this day. Thank you to Bobby Flay for his words of wisdom, Curtis Stone for his support and insight, and Steve Ells for his friendship and advice. To the amazing producers Dan Cutforth, Jane Lipsitz, and Nan Strait, thank you for believing in me and my vision. To Luis Eduardo, devoted friend, without your help, this journey would never have been possible. Craig and Amy Carpentieri, thank you for always enlightening me with your thoughts about life and positivity, and always supporting me in both good and difficult times. To my best friend Juan Carlos Ruiz and Rick and Mina Lieberman, my dearest longtime friends, thanks for staying close to me throughout all these years and for being the best recipe tasters.

I worked with so many people to bring this book to life. Pamela Cannon, my editor at Ballantine, believed in my vision and who I am, not just as a chef but as a person. Thank you for helping me create a voice that is true to myself. To Raquel Pelzel, thank you for putting into written words what I can only voice. Also, thank you to Quentin Bacon, my incredible photographer; Mariana Velasquez, food stylist; and David Asher, props stylist, for having the amazing ability to take my ideas and turn them into beautiful images.

The biggest thank you goes to the United States of America, for giving me the opportunity to represent my Latin culture, my passion, and my ideas each and every day.

RECIPES BY CATEGORY

SOUPS

SALADS

VEGETABLES

DESSERTS

INDEX

Page references in *italics* refer to illustrations.

ABOUT THE AUTHOR

LORENA GARCIA was born and raised in Venezuela, where she completed her law studies. She later moved to the United States to study culinary arts at Johnson & Wales University. After working as an apprentice alongside such world-renowned chefs as Pascal Audin and Gennaro Esposito, she opened two successful Latin-Asian infusion restaurants in Miami, where she currently lives. In spring 2011 she appeared alongside celebrity chefs Bobby Flay and Curtis Stone and Chipotle CEO Steve Ells as a panelist/investor on NBC's new series *America's Next Great Restaurant*. Additionally, she has taken on the challenge of combating childhood obesity with Big Chef, Little Chef, a comprehensive program to help kids and families take control of their eating habits and lives. Garcia opened Lorena Garcia Cocina in February 2011 in the American Airlines terminal at Miami International Airport.

ABOUT THE TYPE

This book was set in Scala Sans, a typeface designed by Martin Majoor in 1991. It was originally designed for a music company in the Netherlands and then was published by the international type house FSI FontShop. Its distinctive extended serifs add to the articulation of the letterforms to make it a very readable typeface.